THE MOUNT CARMEL STORY

1938~2008

ALEXANDRIA, MINNESOTA

Orval K. Moren

THE MOUNT CARMEL STORY
Copyright 2008 by Orval K. Moren, and Mount Carmel Ministries
Published by Mount Carmel Ministries
P. O. Box 579
Alexandria, Minnesota 56308
1-800-793-4311, www.MountCarmelMinistries.com
Printed by CSN Inc. (Christian Services Network)
1975 Janich Ranch Ct
El Cajon, CA 92019
Phone 1-866-484-6184 www.CSNBooks.com
ISBN:978-1-59352-421-0

Acknowledgements

The Mount Camel Story, 1938-2008, celebrating 70 years of ministry to the Lutheran community is compiled and written by Orval Kenneth Moren through interview and research. All the participants are enthusiastically thanked for their time and wonderful cooperation in making the writing of this story and history possible. I thank Peggy Zender, a retired court reporter who transcribed the cassette tapes into words, Nels Hinderlie and Rene Moen for editing, critiquing and suggestions, and Susie Quaas for critiquing the manuscript. Especially I thank my wife, Bernell, for reading the manuscript several times and making helpful suggestions, for encouragement and support.

To honor Philip Jesness, H. J. Stolee, Samuel Miller, Roy Bloomquist, Luther Lerseth, Johan and Sonja Hinderlie, Courtland Agre, and the Proclaimers who have all prayed and believed and supported and upheld Mount Carmel through thick and thin.

Table of Contents

Introduction

Mount Carmel is holy ground for most people who walk its grounds. A certain breath of fresh air gives a feeling of comfort and expectation. A certain peace seems to fall upon the visitors. Many people have expressed a wonderful feeling of familiarity as they pass through the entry gate and begin the slow ascent up the road toward the chapel area. When I come, I am already thinking renewal and relationship among close friends and my Lord. This awesome feeling has been reinforced again and again to me and the hundreds of campers who have attested to this rich spiritual experience and is shared by every family.

The Mount Carmel Story and Chapter One begin with an article first published on May 5, 1982 in the Alexandria Sentinel. It was an interview with Philip Jesness. I have borrowed extensively from that article, as well as expanding upon it with a long interview with Phil in September of 2000, when I began to write this history—The Story.

Over 62 years, Phil was at the camp every week and often every day. Only during WW II was he unable to attend the summer sessions due to gas rationing. Otherwise, Phil said, he was there a few times every year. From the 1960's and into his retirement, he was able to attend regularly. After his retirement, Mount Camel became his life. He had done every thing there was to do at the camp including speaking to groups about the story of Mount Carmel. The article and the interview are Chapter One.

Chapter Two is from an original booklet produced by the Lutheran Bible Institute (LBI) to advertise and tell the story of Mount Carmel. Written by Dr. Samuel Miller, I have copied it as he wrote it.

In Chapter Three I have made additions and corrections to an interview of Dr. Miller by Pastor W. A. Force in 1972. This was necessary because the speech was live and tape-recorded. Some sentences were not complete as we do in conversation. However, the context is there just as it was delivered.

Chapter Four is the writing of Pastor Stolee who wrote about Mount Carmel in the LBI's *Bible Banner*, the school's major publication for the School and the Lutheran community.

The remaining chapters are gathered materials from a variety of sources. These include individual writings, recording of interviews and summary of accounts from articles, periodicals and camp brochures and my own observations.

The book is the Mount Carmel Story. It is not the history. Some of the facts and statistics do not match, and some even may conflict. No attempt has been made to correct what might be construed as mistakes or omissions. It is like standing on a corner watching an exciting parade. Each person on each corner sees something different and exciting. Much more family history and experiences were originally written. However, some was edited out because there simply was too much. Enjoy what you read, and let the Lord bless you as you praise Him.

Chapter One

AN ARTICLE AND INTERVIEW
WITH PHILIP JESNESS

THE BEGINNINGS

On a beautiful spring day, March 22, 1938, I came to Alexandria with a job to help build a new Bible Camp. Spring was everywhere and the farmers were in the fields. But a few days later, winter returned with a fury blocking the road and the dropping the temperature to near zero.

I had been a student at the Lutheran Bible Institute in St. Paul, Minnesota. After completing the course work and graduating from the school in 1937, I worked in the school as a custodian. I had been offered the chance for work in building this new camp, and was tickled to get the job because my girl friend lived close by. I was born in 1911 in Stevens County near Morris, Minnesota.

ORIGINS

The Lutheran Bible Institute opened a school for Bible study in St. Paul in 1919 and ten years later, a new building in Minneapolis. The summer of 1920, LBI started "The summer session of the Lutheran Bible Institute." It is thought that this was the first Bible camp in the Midwest. It was held at a resort on Lake Independence in Maple Plain, Minnesota. Sessions were held there every summer until Mount Carmel opened in 1938.

In 1937, Dr. Samuel Miller, president of the LBI, was told about a 40-acre farm eight miles north of Alexandria on the west side of Lake Carlos. He went to look at the property. The very same day he went to view the farm, the owner—Mr. Fred Bartel was on the premises. Dr. Miller felt this was the answer to their prayers. Mr. Bartel agreed that he would sell the land to the Bible School for $2,500. Dr. Miller brought the LBI staff out to see the property. They gathered for prayer on the highest point and agreed to ask the Board to buy the land. In the fall of 1937, the Board voted to buy the land and to build a camp, but not to spend over $40,000.00.

PLANS WERE DRAWN AND LEADERS SELECTED

Pastor H. J. Stolee was chosen by Dr. Samuel Miller to be the supervisor of the work on what would become a new summer camp to be called Mount Carmel. Thirty seven buildings with a chapel and dining hall were planned. Every cabin was to be the exact same size and shape.

Dr. Miller himself was afraid that the camp would be "too much Miller," so he had taken a sabbatical and arranged for a trip to Palestine. He would be gone for three months. When Dr. Miller returned the camp was totally built and completed.

Pastor Stolee had been placed in complete charge of building the camp. I was his straw boss—his right-hand man. Pastor Stolee planned the projects, and I assigned the men to their jobs day-by-day working right along with the men. Each man received one dollar a day plus room and board as our wages.

How these men were selected and hired, I do not know. But, there were seven young men—Fred Johnson, Martin Mickelson, Ralph Carlson, Clarence Aaland, Oscar Rui, Virgil Lundquist, and, me—Phil Jesness, who were hired to do all the preparatory ground work for the buildings.

CONTRACTORS AND MATERIALS

The contractors were hired. Earl Drusell from Alexandria was the general building contractor. Seven trainloads of lumber and five carloads of cement were shipped to Alexandria and hauled out by the Alexandria Dray Company. The pieces of lumber for each building were cut using hand saws by the carpenters of the building contractor. All the door frames were cut this same way. The doors were hung by use of hammer and hand saw, wood chisel, bit and brace. None of the buildings were finished on the inside.

The Thompson Gravel Company brought out many truck loads. A gasoline driven mixer mixed the cement and gravel into concrete, and we delivered one wheelbarrow full at a time wherever it was needed. Water was pumped from the lake through a small garden hose to the cement mixer by a small gasoline engine.

The Runestone Electric Associates put in the transmission lines and power. Dahlquist Electric furnished all the light poles. We dug the holes for them by hand and set all of the light poles. They have remained where they were set until this day.

Smith and Moen was the plumbing contractor. The plumbers cut and threaded all the water pipes by hand. Ettesvold Well Drilling Company of Morris, Minnesota was hired to drill the six-inch well. Pastor Stolee had selected a spot and had driven in a stake where he thought the well should be dug. But, the well driller pulled up his machine to a spot about 10 feet from the mark Pastor Stolee had made. Stolee suggested the well driller move the stake. He did, and hit water at 90 feet, but he didn't find enough gallons of water in the first hole. He moved the machine and drilled another hole about ten feet away hoping for a better water flow and more gallons of water per minute. He was thinking now he may need to use two wells. But, he hit such a good vein at nearly the same level that it has been pumping sweet clear water for more than 60 years. The pipes from the first drilling were pulled and reused.

PREPARATORY WORK

We seven men did all the preparatory work of cutting unwanted trees, removing the stumps, trimming out the brush, and leveling the ground for the chapel and dining hall. All this work was done with pick and shovel. Scrapers pulled by two or four horses from the local farmers helped with the terracing, especially around the chapel area. No heavy equipment was used—no Caterpillars, only a small grader helped with the leveling. It was pulled by a new 1937 Ford truck purchased for $400.00 in Minneapolis with dual tires and four speed transmission.

The truck had mechanical brakes, which were weak and actually dangerous, because you had to step hard to stop it. One time I was coming from Minneapolis on highway 52. A little boy dashed out into the street in the town of Freeport. I skidded the tires to a stop, and pushed so hard on the brakes that I locked up my knee. The Lord gave me the extra power to stop that loaded truck and save that little boy, who was holding on to the bumper.

When the preparatory work began, the building contractor came out to look over the plans and assess the amount of work to be done. He and Pastor Stolee were standing side by side on the highest mound, just about where the dining hall is today.

The building contractor said to Stolee, "You mean to tell me that these seven men are going to dig all the trenches and complete this leveling, and I have a deadline for this project? What if I have to wait for these guys to catch up? What then?"

Pastor Stolee replied, (I know what he said, because I was standing right beside him as he spoke), "If these men hold you up for even one hour, you will get a day, and if they hold you up for a whole day, you will get eight extra days of contract pay at the end of the project."

I looked at Pastor Stolee and thought to myself, "What in the world are you doing to us?" But, I tell you that Virgil and Ralph could dig a cesspool six feet across and eight feet deep in one working day.

Nine large cesspools for the restrooms and kitchen, and 29 smaller ones were dug by hand. Each cabin had a small cesspool about five feet deep filled with rock and stones for good drainage so that the dirty sink water drained into an individual cesspool.

Each cabin had running water and a sink. Five rest rooms were built also with toilets for campers and public use. Two major rest rooms—called comfort stations, with hot water shower stalls were built centrally located with one end of the building for the men and the other for the women. The water for the showers was heated by a wood and coal heater. When the heater got too hot, even the cold water in the toilet was warm.

Approximately one mile of trenches was dug for the water lines and footings for the cabins. About 1500 feet of trenches, (one foot wide and two and a half feet deep) were dug for the chapel and dining hall. We workers spread the dirt from the trenches for the buildings and we never lost even five minutes of contract time. The camp was to be completed by June 15, 1938 with running water and electricity and the contractors were gone by that date. The total cost was $40,000.00.

Then preparations were made so that Mount Carmel as a Bible Camp could open July 2. Food was prepared and served day by day for all the workers and volunteers. It was like a testing to determine how things were working. There were many people who were making arrangements in the dining hall, housekeeping units, the cabins, and the chapel.

When Mount Carmel was built, all the open area was field—the land was a farm. The Olson brothers came and worked the ground with their horses and seeded in the fields with oats and grass seed. The oats acted as a cover crop to protect the new grass seed. This made it into a meadow. Farmers came late that summer and fall to cut the hay for use on their farms.

Malcom Borgendale, the custodian at the LBI, came up and worked to make the grounds into lawns. He picked up the stones on the fields, began to cut the grass with a hand mower, and expanded the lawn area. When Mount Carmel was able to get tractors for lawn mowing, all the fields were turned into lawns, but this took a few years.

HOUSING AND FOOD FOR THE SEVEN OF US

All seven of us men stayed at the Arthur Olson farm home. Myrtle Olson and her husband Arthur lived on the farm down the road to the west. The Olson house was two miles west of Mount Carmel. The gravel road curved around the lake. Right there is where the farmstead was. That gravel road passed by what is now Luther Crest, where the new big houses are built.

The house had four bedrooms upstairs. It was cozy. We ate all of our meals prepared by that wonderful woman, Myrtle Olson. She received one dollar a day per man for three meals a day. Her meals were well prepared and with large portions. We were fed well.

There was no running water in the house so we had a wash basin and water in the upstairs hallway, and an outdoor toilet. But, there was no place at the house for a bath. Pastor Stolee solved that by bringing a wash tub to the camp. We cleaned up in the main cabin at camp on Saturdays, as there was a working well on the grounds with a hand pump for fresh water.

STOLEE DINING HALL AND THE KITCHEN

All the tables and chairs for the dining room came from a furniture company in Minneapolis. I hauled up all the furnishings, truck load after truck load, from there on highway 52 now highway 10 through St. Cloud. Sometimes I was so tired while driving I couldn't even remember going through a town. I was sleeping as I was driving—I think an angel was driving and protecting me.

The kitchen had a large oil burning range which also heated the water for the kitchen. The walk-in cooler was cooled with ice. The cabins and canteen also had ice boxes as they were cheap to buy. I remember when we picked up the iceboxes at the Butler Brothers Warehouse in St. Paul, how they dug them out of a corner where they were covered with dust. The company was glad to see them go. The iceboxes served for eight years until electric refrigeration was put in the kitchen, and then all the housekeeping cabins got refrigerators too.

The cooks in the kitchen at the LBI in Minneapolis came out to the camp in the summer. But later, Mount Carmel hired its own cooks just for the summer. As an example, when Hub (Hubert) Malm was the camp director, his wife, Evelyn, was the head cook. This also occurred with Roy and Marge Bloomquist.

The dining hall was always a special place and there was no fooling around in it. The ladies were required to wear a dress in the dining hall. The dining hall meals were served by waitresses who also had special dresses for their task. Many of them had been students at the LBI, and working in the dining room was their summer job. The girls who worked in the dining hall and who cleaned the cabins lived in the two cabins next to the dining hall. Sometimes, there were nine girls in those two cabins. They were packed in like sardines.

I was never allowed in the dining hall for a meal because I was never properly dressed. I usually had my old work clothes on. Instead, I ate in the little room just off to the right of the back door to the kitchen. All of us workers ate in that little room. It was later used for the freezers. We didn't care where we ate because the cooks were really good to us. We all ate "like pigs," big portions of food and good, too. This happened in the early years.

After I was married to Marie, she helped out in many different tasks as well. Her work was gratis and she never received anything, nor did she want it. But that was a little ridiculous as I think about it now.

STORE AND GASOLINE PUMP

Often those living around the area came for meat, bread, milk, and fruit. Mount Carmel had a store and sold groceries and supplies, which had been planned for from the very beginning. The store was there from opening day on July 2 and was located in the corner next to the kitchen near the canteen. The store was not there for profit and in fact, the camp probably just broke even on it. The bread truck and milk truck each came out every other day. People who were doing the housekeeping needed to buy basic groceries without going into town.

Dr. Miller had a little bigger vision for the camp than just Bible Study. He wanted comfort and opportunity for everyone. And, of course, the canteen with soda pop and candy and popcorn was there for treats every night.

The Skelly Oil Company had a 500-gallon underground gasoline tank and pump for the camp. Actually, Mount Carmel sold a lot of gasoline as well as groceries, and eventually the camp bought the tank and pump. The gas pump was located near the garage and is now a collector's item. The old pump is still there as you can see, but the tank was removed many years ago.

GARAGE AND WELL HOUSE AND ICE HOUSE

The water pressure tank and pump were out in the open on a permanent concrete slab. Pressure for the water system came through a 2500 gallon holding tank. The tank was purchased in St. Paul and delivered to the camp by the manufacturer. The large capacity of the water tank enabled the camp to always have a supply of water even when the electricity failed. Because of the large size, which meant water could be pumped slowly, the well itself has remained good. A garage was built around the water tank in the fall of 1938. The garage had not been in the original contract. Fred Johnson and I built that building.

In the fall of 1938, Fred Johnson and I also built an icehouse, and that icehouse was filled for the next seven years in the wintertime. That building is now the storage shed between the housekeeping cabins and the garage.

Arthur Olson had the equipment to cut ice from the lake and a crew of men lifted the blocks of ice. We used our truck to haul the blocks up to the icehouse, banked them with sawdust and completed the ice harvest. This was done in the month of February when the ice was frozen thick. We also filled four or five other small icehouses for other homeowners around the lake.

After the ice harvest, I would trim trees, cut wood, and remove brush. There were many things to keep me busy. Heavy snowfalls those first years, and keeping the roofs shoveled off was a major job in itself.

CABINS AND HOUSEKEEPING CABINS

The cost to stay a week in the guest cabin including board was $12. The campers could use the housekeeping cabins with eight people for $15 or $25 for the whole family per week. There were ten housekeeping cabins and they were always full. Each cabin had an icebox, stove, table and chairs. Of course, they had to do their own cooking and housekeeping. They could eat in the dining hall, but most didn't have the money for that luxury. The program was, as it is now, Bible centered in all the sessions and recreation included everyone.

MILLER CHAPEL

The chapel had multiple uses from the beginning. Campers gathered in it for all the Bible studies and for worship services. All the meetings were held there as well. In the early days, there were three worship services every Sunday—one in the morning, one in the afternoon at 3:00 p.m. and another in the evening. The men were expected to wear a shirt, tie, and a coat. Likewise, ladies were asked to wear dresses at worship services.

One mid-summer Sunday afternoon worship service was especially warm inside even with the fans running. On that Sunday, I recall, Pastor Stolee broke the rule. He was speaking, and he said, "I am taking off my coat." In a few minutes, there wasn't a man with his suit coat on. From that time on, the men would come in their shirtsleeves.

The pews in the chapel were built and delivered from a sash and door company in Fergus Falls. They came unassembled, unfinished, unstained and unvarnished. We did all that work as a part of the preparation for the opening day. In the second year in the winter, I made all the book racks for the songbooks in the chapel. I used a jigsaw for each rack. I cut out each one, one at a time, and placed them on the chapel pews just as they are today.

The dinner bell used for opening day was a hand bell similar to one that a teacher used for classrooms. However, the camp was opened only a few days when a man came asking for help to unload a beautiful brass bell from a Northern Pacific railroad locomotive. This fellow was an engineer on the railroad and his identity is unknown. The little bell from the train is mounted in the tower by the dining hall. The other bell that hangs by the Miller Chapel is a church bell. Its origin is unknown. I say, "May the bells continue to ring."

One of the dreams of Dr. Miller was an amphitheater. His dream was to put it where we now have the new amphitheater. Another dream and goal was that Mount Carmel be a winterized camp so that it might have year round use.

The cross that is lit up by night outside the front of the chapel near the lake shore was added many years later. It is not very old. But it can be seen from across the lake. Many people on the lake use the cross as a directional spot on the lake. What better way to find your way than looking for the lighted cross.

OFFICE AND REGISTRATION CABIN

One cabin was insulated and became our winter residence. Fred Johnson and I stayed there the first winter of 1938. Fred stayed until Christmas. Snowstorms were common and the road was frequently blocked for two or three days. Early in the fall of 1939, we added a room to the cabin which was to be our bedroom. That cabin was to become my home for five years.

In 1940, the entry porch was added which became our kitchen. In the summer we used an electric plate for cooking. In the winter we had a small 3/4 size wood burning range with an oven, which Pastor Stolee had brought up. Pastor Stolee thought of everything. Also in 1940, I built a shed as a barn for a cow so that we could have a daily supply of milk.

In the summer we had running water, but in the winter I pumped it from the well. Marie and I stayed in that cabin until 1943 when we decided to move into Alexandria for work with the war. Then the cabin became the office for registration and administration.

THE WAR YEARS

I married Marie Stark on Saturday, September 3, 1939. The next day, while we were honeymooning in Little Falls, MN, we heard on the radio that Germany had invaded Poland. We were married the day WW II started. I was then 28 years old and a married man so I was not immediately selected for the draft. But my time for work in the war effort would come.

Our first child—Phyllis Marie, a baby girl was born the next year, prematurely. She lived only three days. Our second child—Karl, was born in November 1941 in the hospital in Alexandria. Our third child—Lenore, was born two years later.

I was forced to leave Mount Carmel in 1943, after being there for five years because the Draft Board said I had to work in an essential industry. The Nelson Creamery needed help, so I learned how to make butter. A lot of the butter I made went to the South Pacific war area. Later, I went to work for the Carlson Dairy where I bottled milk and made ice cream. My last seven years of work was at the Douglas County Hospital as an engineer. It was the first time I worked only an eight hour day!

During the war years, 1942-44, many of the campers were office girls—single girls and war widows who needed a vacation and time to rethink their lives. Their boy friends and husbands were gone in the war. They came by train or bus to Alexandria and to Mount Carmel. We would pick them up with our Ford Station wagon. They paid 25 cents per person by day and 50 cents in the evening for this taxi service.

In 1942, the war caused rationing for everyone. Campers were encouraged to bring sugar, which was the first to be rationed, or stamps that could be used for rationing. Cheese, butter, meat and gasoline were all rationed. Because of a lack of sugar, ice cream, pop and candy were limited. But, with the help of the local bottlers, we had pop, and the North American Creamery helped with ice cream and candy. The gasoline rationing deeply affected camp attendance. I got help in gas rationing from the Skelly dealer who was a Baptist, and I really appreciated his act of kindness toward our Camp.

KNOCK YOUTH CHAPEL

In the spring of 1945, LBI received a large tent that was to be used by the youth as a chapel. It was set up where the white house for the caretaker is now located. In 1950, the Youth Chapel was built by Martin Mickelson who was one of the original seven Mount Carmel work crew. Because A. W. Knock paid for most of it, the Youth Chapel was named the Knock Chapel in his honor.

TREES, SHRUBS AND FLOWERS

In the beginning, the land had been a farm so there were only a few trees. Some maple and ash trees grew along the ridge, and some others stood around the chapel area. And of course, there was a shoreline of trees. All the evergreen trees we now see were planted under the supervision of Pastor Knock. The rows of evergreens that line the driveway coming in up the hill were planted by First Lutheran Church Boy Scouts in the early 1950's. They were seedlings, about six inches high.

There is an interesting story about the evergreens that are near the chapel and the dining hall. A lady in Minnetonka had some acreage, with small seedlings—about a foot tall, growing in a swamp area. She told Pastor Knock that he could come and dig them out and replant them. They inquired with a nurseryman how to do it. He said such a plan was impossible, and that they would never grow. But, Pastor Knock was not convinced. He wanted to try to replant them, and he assigned us to do it!

Fred Johnson and I went down to Minneapolis with the truck one day. We dug up a truckload, about thirty trees. The pastors who were here that day dug the holes just where Pastor Knock wanted them planted, along the road by the chapel and the dining hall. They are the big evergreens we now see.

Pastor Knock tried to grow a vegetable garden, but it didn't work out. When the Mattsons were caretakers, they tried to grow a vegetable garden. But it was too much work and not enough produce to make the gardens worthwhile. He usually planted the flower gardens although I am not sure where he got all of the flowers in the early years.

Later on Pastor Knock, together with a nurseryman from Fertile, Minnesota, named Melvin Bergeson, made flower gardens in several places. Apparently they had met during one of Pastor Knock's Bible Conferences in northern Minnesota, and had become good friends. That friendship lasted for many years. Every spring around Memorial Day, Bergeson would come with a carload of flowers. In later years, his son came with flowers, and now the grandson brings the same flowers. Not only have they supplied flowers, but they have also supplied Mount Carmel with many of the new shrubs and some trees.

LAKE CARLOS

When Mount Carmel was built, the water level in Lake Carlos was so low that we could drive a truck along the south shore and beach area. It was from that shore area that we took a lot of the rock and stone that was used in the buildings. In that south shore area, there was a large rock with a natural colored cross embedded into the face of the stone. But when the rains came, the south beach was lost to high water and ice. The high water level and the ice buried that famous stone with the picture of the cross along the south shore somewhere. The swimming area was moved east to the location where it is now.

There was a sign at the beach which said, "No swimming on Sunday." Whenever anyone went to the beach, they had to wear a long beach robe or a housecoat to walk to the beach area. The men would wear a long coat or slip on their pants and shirt. No one was to walk beyond the beach in a bathing suit. Dr. Miller made the rules. He said, "No smoking!" But, if someone needed to smoke they were to go away to the low area. Dr. Miller would say, "If God had intended people to smoke, there would have been a chimney."

LAND USE AND THE AREA WEST OF THE CHAPEL

In December 29, 1952, Mount Carmel acquired four acres of land between Mount Carmel and the entrance road as a gift from Miles Vickerman who owned the land. In 1956, Mount Carmel purchased 35 acres of land that was between Mount Carmel and Luther Crest Bible Camp. The land had a house which had been the summer home of Mr. Swenson, who lived in Missouri. He was born on the farm directly across from Luther Crest. He sold the property along with the summer house for $10,000.

The building that is now used for the staff toward the west of the chapel was built in 1940 as a guest cabin for people who wanted to stay a day or two. Charges were one dollar per night if you furnished your own bedding and two dollars if you rented the camp's bedding.

Three pastors were assigned for a given week. Usually they were Miller, Stolee, Knock, Gornitzka, Randolph, and Anderson. The pastors who ran the camp for the week stayed in the three cabins to the west. They each had a cabin, but they were very small with only a single bed. The pastors were not to bring their families so their wives stayed home in Minneapolis and St. Paul, where they lived. They were not to be distracted from their duties so there was no time to be bothered with wives and children. But, really there was no place for them to sleep on the west side.

Dr. Miller broke the rule in the third year when he bought a little camper trailer for him and his wife to stay in. He put it west of the chapel. They both liked the idea of a camper trailer, so then Dr. Miller bought a very large trailer house for him and his wife. When A. B. Anderson came up with his family, they would stay up the hill in a house which they rented.

Six cabins, numbers 4-9, were purchased in 1956 and moved from the Lake Ida area to the area west of the chapel. The cabins had been part of a resort on Lake Ida, which was closed and sold. Many improvements were made by volunteers and helpers.

FINANCIAL PROBLEMS

Mount Carmel was used as collateral on a loan by the college to sustain the college program. This resulted in the Lutheran Bible Institute being unable to make payments for its loans on the mortgage and caused Mount Carmel deep financial trouble. The other financial problem was the sewer system.

In 1977, the entire lake area was connected to the Alexandria sanitary sewer system, including Mount Carmel. It was mandated! The camp had two years to complete the work. Roy Bloomquist, the director at that time, along with his wife Marge, saw Mount Carmel through some rather hard years. Probably, Roy had the hardest time because he was operating against the debt of the college. He had no money to work with. To pay for the sewer project, he got a three-year note at five percent interest from the bank in Alexandria. The cost for hooking up the entire camp to the sewer line cost approximately $35,000. Each cabin was replumbed and new toilets and showers installed.

Roy went out and raised the money. He had it deposited in the bank in Alexandria. The college wanted the money, but Roy would not let go of it. Instead, he paid off the note and saved Mount Carmel. The years 1985, 1986 and 1987 became landmark years. It was make or break time for Mount Carmel, not only with finances, but also with buildings and programming. In 1986 a decision was made to form a corporation for Mount Carmel alone and raise money to save the camp from foreclosure.

But the financial problems continued. The camp actually was locked into a huge debt. The debt was eating up the possibility of improvements, as well as cutting into the current operations. The monies that should have gone to the camp had been siphoned off to the college.

A man named Courtland Agre, whom I knew quite well at Mount Carmel, a retired chemist and college professor from St. Olaf College and Augsburg College came with his wife, Ellen, as a guest to the camp. Courtland would come and scrap old paint and repaint the cabins. He and I talked about the financial debt which seemed to bother him a lot.

One day Courtland Agre came up to me and said, "Phil, we are going to have to create a miracle to get this camp debt paid off." I agreed but what should we do? Dr. Agre came with a surprise challenge to the campers. He had been inspired in the morning worship hour to challenge the worshippers. Johan Hinderlie knows the whole story. It was a total miracle for Mount Carmel. What Agre did was to make a promise a gift of money and ask the campers to match it.

Sure enough! said Phil. In the next two weeks, the guests who came to camp matched the offers. The campers went to work among them selves, and by the end of the first week and the next week had raised matching dollars. Was I surprised? No, I was not! I had seen so many things happen in my years at Mount Carmel, that nothing really surprised me any more! I think the person who was a bit skeptical was Johan.

Maybe he wasn't surprised about Dr. Agre's offer as I think Dr. Agre had spoken to him about the challenge. But the huge amount of matching money, Johan wondered about! Then along came another surprise. Two men heard about what had happened and were inspired to help by giving a matching pledge. Their challenge was something like this, "We have $25,000 each, so lets do it again! If you—meaning Mount Carmel, can match the $50,000 again in the next two weeks, we have this offer for the Camp." I am not free to tell their names.

COURTLAND AGRE WAS GOD'S MAN

Phil's comment was that Dr. Courtland Agre was God's man for the time. I really don't know what inspired him to do that, said Phil. In my own life, I have had very little money. My role in all of this was to be an encourager to Dr. Agre and to Johan, and the others.

STRONG LEADERSHIP, DEDICATED WORKERS AND VOLUNTEERS

From the very beginning and over the years, Mount Carmel has had dedicated workers, wonderful volunteers, and strong leadership. The camp directors have been: Pr. Stolee, Alvar Nelson, Pr. Hubert Malm, Pr. Roy Bloomquist, Pr. Luther Lerseth, and Pr. Johan Hinderlie. Hundreds of people have been involved with Mount Carmel through the years. Many people— kitchen staff and dining hall table waitresses, youth workers and pastors, caretakers, volunteers and many others have helped with the programming.

The first men on the work crew set the example and they went on to a good life—Fred Johnson continued working as a carpenter, Martin Mickelson also became a carpenter, Ralph Carlson became a plumber, Clarence Aaland and Oscar Rui started farming, Virgil Lundquist became a pastor. And me—Phil Jesness? I stayed in the area with my dearly beloved Marie. By the spring of 1999, only three of us were living, and my beloved Marie was gone as well!

In 1950, Arvid Mattson became the caretaker. He built the present white house in 1954 at a cost of $7,000. In 1956, a basement and bathroom were added. The Farmall tractor that was used for many years came through Arvid. Other caretakers besides me were Richard Haufek, The Mattsons, Les Larson, The Smiths, Jerry and Jan Lang, and most recently Marvin Nysetvold. Mount Carmel has always had good strong maintenance and caretakers.

I consider myself fortunate to have been in contact with Mount Carmel for all these 60 plus years of work and encouragement. I have been greatly blessed.

DEAR FRIENDS OF MOUNT CARMEL,

On this past Sunday afternoon, October 16, 2005, our dear friend and partner in ministry, Philip Jesness fell asleep in the Lord for his last time. At 94 years old Phil knew that his days on this earth were reaching an end.

Phil was joined in marriage to Marguerite Bachman a few years ago at Mount Carmel and she was with him at the very end. She told me, "He slept away. He was very peaceful." The two of them had been living in a care center called the Clearwater Estates in Alexandria.

Phil was a member of a team of 8 men who helped clear the ground in 1938 for the preparation of Mount Carmel. He lived here year-round as the first caretaker with his family. Phil served here as a volunteer for over 18 years following the death of his first wife. We often called on him as our "Historian."

He was my guide in many situations especially helping in understanding the continuity between our current ministry and that of LBI.

We will miss Phil. He was a man of incredible wisdom and depth. His memory for events and situations at Mount Carmel was profound. He helped all of us live more fully for the Lord.

We bless the memory of Phil Jesness. He reminds me of the calling that John the Baptist had: He came as a witness, to bear witness about the light, that all might believe through him. He was not the light, but came to bear witness about the light. John 1:7-8

With thanksgiving for this man sent from God,

Yours in Christ,
Johan Hinderlie

Chapter Two

MOUNT CARMEL...HOPES AND PRAYERS

This chapter was written by Dr. Samuel Miller, and published as a Booklet in 1938. No changes have been made except for the computer generated punctuation corrections.

"This is the story of how the Lutheran Bible Institute obtained the beautiful forty acres on the shores of Lake Carlos in Douglas County, eight miles north of Alexandria, Minnesota, now called "Mount Carmel," the home of the summer session of the Lutheran Bible Institute.

For many years, we had hoped and prayed for a home of our own for the summer sessions. God had granted us great blessings at Lake Independence. But because the property was not our own, and because we had to share it with others, it was not possible to do many things that we wanted to do at our summer sessions. For three years we also rented quarters at Lake Geneva, near Alexandria. This gave us opportunity to become acquainted with that part of our State and to look around at possible sites.

TIME FOR DECISION

In the Summer of 1937, the Spirit of God was strongly moving in the hearts of all of us connected with the L. B. I. that the time had come when we should make some definite decision concerning a place of our own. We examined many sites. Next to the Lake Geneva Bible Camp, which we were renting, there were two pieces of property, each twenty acres. We found that the two pieces could be purchased for about $10,000. There were certain drawbacks, especially the proximity to the Lake Geneva Bible Camp. But we liked the territory, and other sites that we had examined cost just as much, and even more.

One morning I was going to the Court House in Alexandria to get information which would lead to more definite steps of purchase. On the street I met the secretary of the Chamber of Commerce, who knew that we were looking for a site, and he inquired as to the progress we were making. When I told him that we would have to pay about $100 an acre for the ground, he said, "Those people do not want to sell their property. You can buy property for much less than that."

He then told me that the State had purchased the property at the northern end of Lake Carlos for a State Park, and that there was a forty-acre piece next to what the State had purchased, which they were trying to purchase but the owner wanted more than the State would pay. "If you will offer them $1,000 for the forty acres, I feel sure that they will take it," he said. "And we who are working for the State Park will have no objection to the Lutheran Bible Institute occupying that piece."

PRAYER FOR GUIDANCE

Before I went that morning, I had definitely prayed to God that every step that I took that day should be in the guidance of the Holy Spirit. I, therefore, dared not disregard this advice that had come to me all unexpectedly. I immediately drove out to the land that he had indicated, but found that it was not suitable, being very low and swampy, without an attractive shore that could be used for a bathing beach.

But while I was standing there looking about, I met another man who had a cottage and some property nearby. I found that he was fully familiar with all the land around the lake, and I asked him if he knew of any place that might be a suitable place for a camp. Without my telling him, he said, "You must be from the Lutheran Bible Institute."

"How do you know that?" I said.

"Oh," he answered, "it is known all about here that you are looking for a site."

Then he told me about a piece of ground, which he said a Mr. Bartel had been trying to sell to him. He described the location and said, "You look it over, but look out for the owner. He will certainly try to get as much out of you as he possibly can."

THE LAND IS FOUND

Praying to God all the time for guidance, I now looked up this piece of ground, and was fortunate enough to find the owner, Mr. Bartel, on the grounds. He was working on the very highest point of the rolling hills overlooking the lake. As I walked up the hill, I was immediately struck with the marvelous beauty of the location. Before I even entered into conversation with Mr. Bartel, I said to myself, "This is where the dinning-room and lobby should be. And over on this other knoll is where the chapel ought to be."

I found Mr. Bartel very talkative. He soon told me that he was a member of the Lutheran Church (Missouri Synod) in Alexandria, and was very friendly indeed. When I asked him if he would like to sell the piece of property upon which he was working, he said, "Well, yes, but you would not pay what I want for it." After much conversation, he had told me that he had paid $2,500 for the forty acres, that not long ago he had been offered $3,500 for it, but had held (on to) it in the hope that he could obtain more. Now, he said, he realized that he was getting old, that values had gone down and he would be glad if he could get out of it what he had put into it.

"Suppose, then," I said, "that we offered you $2,500 for it. Would that attract you at all?" Without hesitation he answered, "Yes, to you folks, I would be glad to sell it for $2,500. It has yielded enough crops," he said, "to pay for the taxes and a little income besides, and I will be satisfied if I get out of it what I have put in it."

OPINIONS UNITED

With enthusiasm, I went back to the friends and coworkers at L. B. I. and told them, I had found the site for our summer home. But, to my surprise, when they came to see the land, hardly any of them liked it. One or two agreed with me that it was very beautiful, that it would make a fine site for our summer session. But most of them shook their heads. When members of the Board of Trustee came to see the place, they had the same reaction. They felt that the hills were too high and that there were not enough woods on the grounds.

Personally, I felt that I had been guided by God, but that I should not argue the matter. I told the friends, "I will not try to persuade you, but let us wait and see what the Lord will reveal to us." It was an interesting experience to see how little by little the minds were changed. As the friends went and looked at the place again and again, they began to realize that it would indeed be a beautiful site. So all were agreed and the Board of Trustees decided that the land should be purchased at the price that Mr. Bartel had accepted. We found Mr. Bartel very fine to deal with, scrupulously correct and honest.

GROUND CLAIMED

In September of 1937, the faculty was given the use of a cabin on nearby Lake Darling for a couple of days, and we looked over the ground that we felt the Lord had given us. On the highest knoll, near where there is now a rock garden and a covered terrace overlooking the lake, we had out first faculty prayer meeting. There we claimed that ground in the Name of the Lord Jesus for the Lutheran Bible Institute and prayed that we might be enabled to build the necessary buildings thereon.

BUILDINGS PLANNED AND ERECTED

It became a busy fall and winter planning the structures, and in the early spring of 1938, Pastor H. J. Stolee assumed the task and heavy burden of supervising the construction. In answer to our prayers, God gave him special guidance and strength so that he was enabled to build the beautiful Mount Carmel, to which we now may invite those who want to come and spend some time in the summer in the study of the Word of God. We had the money to pay for the land. Friends of L. B. I. loaned the money to build the buildings, the total investment being about $40,000.

THE NAME

The name Mount Carmel? It was chosen to be identification and a challenge. Like Mount Carmel in Palestine, it is a beautiful highland overlooking a body of water. Here the Word of God challenges all who come to make a wholehearted surrender of themselves to the living God, and the fire of the Holy Spirit continues to fall on the sacrifice on many who present themselves unto God in the Name of Jesus Christ our Lord.

Rates Room and board in the cabins for four persons...$10.00 and $12.00 per week.

Housekeeping cabins for eight persons...$15.00 per week.

Registration fee...$2.00 per person per week.

Study 10 One-week Courses in June, July, and August

Chapter Three

Bible Banner Article H. J. Stolee

In September of 1938, H. J. Stolee wrote a lengthy article titled "Mount Carmel" for the Lutheran Bible Institute's, *Bible Banner*, which was the school's main publication for distribution to the supporters of the Lutheran Bible Institute. Pastor Stolee had been the supervisor of the building of Mount Carmel during the spring and summer of 1938. The story that follows is his writing as published. No changes have been made except the punctuation which the computer has generated.

Mount Carmel, Fall of 1938

"The summer sessions of 1938 are soon finished. At this writing there are only eight days left and the story of the first summer at Mount Carmel will be history. So we are near enough to the closing session now to look back at the eight weeks, to review and to evaluate the summer's work. That, however is not the object of this writing, except as it might be incidental. Yes, only about one week left, and there is every reason to believe that it will be much like the preceding in attendance, in program and we may trust, also in fruits for the Owner of the Vineyard. If the Lord permits, there will be ten weeks of such work at Mount Carmel next year, beginning about the middle of June.

Now we want to talk over this business of summer school with you who were here this year. Let us not forget the hills and lake and woods for a moment, and let us take an inventory of the spiritual gain. Are we taking too much for granted, speaking of the results as a gain? Surely, the results were either negative or positive, either a loss or a gain to you.

Were you among those expecting a season of spiritual refreshing? Then I believe you went home quickened and gladdened. If it be that you were disappointed in teachers and other associates, bring your disappointment and heartache to Him who alone gives rest to weary souls. Or were you, perhaps, among those who came, being bewildered concerning your standing before God? If so, I do hope we made the way of salvation so plain and so inviting that you entered and are now found in Him who is the Way.

Perhaps there were those, too, at Mount Carmel, present only because their folks wanted them there. Were you one of them? Did our regulations and standards irk you? Did the teaching and preaching and praying give you "a pain in the neck"? Well, perhaps I should add that if such were your condition, the Holy Spirit intended that His word should indeed give you pain— in the heart. Will you not make an appointment with the Great Physician? He has diagnosed your case; He can treat you and heal you.

In speaking of benefits, which we sincerely hope every one of you enjoyed, may I mention a "recipe for a happy week at Bible Camp." This is not original with me and I am certain it will not fail. It is plain and practical advice on how to use an hour and a half each day while here. Copy it, and try it next year. Or, better still, try it now in your own neighborhood. Here it is: "Spend half an hour daily letting God speak to you when you read the Bible; spend half an hour speaking to God in prayer; spend half an hour speaking to someone else about God."

When you return to Mount Carmel next year, we hope that the interview rooms at the rear of the chapel need not be used for storerooms, but that you may there find a place to plead with God for your own peace or for the blessing upon some one dear to you. I do hope that you shall also be able to find a bench or a seat under some tree, in the grove or down toward the lakeshore that may be to you a place of quiet retreat. We are sorry that such places were not in readiness for you this year.

We hardly dared to look for a large attendance this year. But we have been happily surprised. Excepting the first two weeks, the place has been filled to capacity. Many have been turned away because we could not give them lodging during the week they wanted to come. In this connection may I say a word that perhaps will sound unpleasant to a few? You know the capacity of this new place is limited. Therefore we urged our friends to make reservations. Now the unpleasant and unfair thing is that some make reservations but do not come. The last minute cancellations are a loss to everybody. You see it is not possible to reach those who would gladly have occupied your room, if you give us notice so late. The others have them made other plans. It is a spiritual loss to them, a financial loss to L.B.I., and may also be a moral loss to you if you acted in an irresponsible manner. To be sure something unforeseen may have happened at the last minute to upset your plans, but much of this kind of annoyance and loss can be avoided. All things therefore whatsoever ye would that men should do unto you, even so do ye also unto them.

There were a number of unfinished items at Mount Carmel this year, and we are grateful that you were patient about those matters. Not every shelf and hook and mirror was in its place. Not every snag and stump and weed cut away. And there is much left undone on the lakeshore and hillside. All this is a part of the "pioneering." It will be better next summer, although some of these improvements will necessarily take time rather than effort or expense. Then, too, we have not forgotten that you will look for a boat pier and diving board, a tennis court, and other arrangements for recreation when you return in 1939. Perhaps someone will give us a boost in these things. Those of you who were here during the first few weeks may not have forgotten the excitement over the roaches, the fragrant (?) pillows, and the powerless electric power. Now we have reason to believe that these will be things of the past.

Need we tell you that your pleasure, so often expressed, over the well-ventilated chapel and comfortable chapel seats has added much to our pleasure? Your appreciation of the inviting dining room and lobby, as well as the compliments on the arrangements in the cabins and cottages, and not the least that you so frequently said about the flowers in the window-boxes and on the grounds—for all this we sincerely thank you. We do hope it shall not be necessary to put you in crowded quarters next year such as some of you had this summer. Of course, we want many here, but, not more than can be housed comfortably.

The L.B.I. administration, trustees, faculty, staff and employees unite in heartfelt thanks to our gracious Heavenly Father and to you for pleasant and blessed fellowship at Mount Carmel this year. The Lord watched over us and protected from harm, epidemic, and calamity. It is our prayer that future years shall find us all uncompromising against every "Baal" and boldly taking our stand for the Lord of Host. There shall then be the "sound of abundance of rain."

MOUNT CARMEL, FALL OF 1943

Dr. Stolee continued. "For years L.B.I. carried on its summer work in rented quarters. Much work, with eternal fruitage, was done. But to be in rented places is necessarily circumscribed in various ways. Naturally then, the matter of having a permanent summer home of our own was made an object of much prayer and planning. So it came about that in the summer of 1937, the Dean of the Institute went scouting around for a suitable place and discovered a forty-acre tract of land for sale on the northwest shore of Lake Carlos. It was a case of love at first sight with him. Some of the rest of us did not see much loveliness, only barren hills covered with stubble and weeds, a grove or two with good trees but also much brush. A fringe of timber along the steep bank of the lake, rocks and stumps where the buildings ought to be.

But with a second look and on second thought, we saw the possibilities. The distance from the city was right for the best Bible Camp life. There was a half mile of lakeshore and the water was clean and cool, and the lake was large enough for good bathing, boating and fishing.

In the fall of 1937, the land was bought for $2,500.00. We wanted to be settled there for work the next summer. There was no place for guests, no place to eat, no place to have meetings. There was no light and no water. The approximate building sites were soon selected. That was as far as we had proceeded at the beginning of the school year 1937-38. During the fall and winter, house plans were made and re-made, and finally blueprinted. Contracts were let for constructing the buildings, for the entire plumbing system and for electric wiring to comply with the specifications of the newly established R. E. A. Telephone lines had to be built, a deep well was to be drilled and pumping equipment installed.

The Board of Trustees had several meetings. Its executive committee conferred every month and the building committee met many times. The project also required real team work on the part of the faculty, the office staff and other employees. All contract jobs were to be completed before June 10.The general oversight was left to the undersigned. Furthermore, empty buildings would not do. Cabin furniture, blankets and linens, kitchen and dining room equipment, chapel seats, boats, a truck—these were some of the obvious purchases. Scores of other items that go to make up a "home" had to be added.

An important factor in our building program was time. Late in March, our "ground crew" began to clear away rocks and stumps. Carloads of lumber and truckloads of cement, gravel, steel and sewer pipes were heaped up near the muddy building sites. At times, more than thirty men were employed, carpenters, plumbers, electrician's, well-drillers, and our own "common laborers." And the marvel is that all the contracts were completed on time. We "moved in" early in July. "We" were some of the teachers, some of the office girls and a number of other young folks, who came to clean windows, scrub floors, paint chairs, hang curtains, wash kitchen utensils, tack up a few screens and trample down some brush and weeds. Then came July 17, the day of dedication. A large congregation joined us in singing, "Now Thank We All Our God."

MOUNT CARMEL COMPLETED

Pastor Stolee continued to write. "Now Mount Carmel is a beauty spot. Sightseers are agreed on that. Few Bible Camps have better equipment or a better location. No stumps or stones now, but acres of greensward. Several hundred planted trees and large flower beds give the grounds a park-like appearance. The native trees have been trimmed and most of the brush is gone. There is still enough left of the "forest primeval" to give the hills a vacation land atmosphere.

Forty-three buildings, some small, some large, all glistening white—several of these added since 1938—make Mount Carmel an attractive community.

The place is not perfect in every detail, but it is clean without being "cityfied." At present, only about one-third of the land is used for lawns, playgrounds and gardens. There is ample space for future expansion."

MOUNT CARMEL TOMORROW

"Hitherto hath the Lord provided. Therefore, we are called to press on. Mount Carmel is not a venture in real estate. It will perhaps never be a "paying proposition," nor is it intended to be merely another camp, a pleasant place for vacations. Mount Carmel's purpose is to afford opportunity for a specialized service in the Church of Jesus Christ. Nothing is too good for the Church; nothing outside of the Church is much good.

Much remains to be done. Some things are urgently needed; in other things we may make haste slowly. Here are some of the "musts," as the undersigned sees them.

Improvement of the road near our grounds.

A better roof on the two main buildings, (this is the urgent item for 1944).

Improvements in the housekeeping cottages and moving some of them to new sites.

A small youth chapel.

Then, too, we have dreams for the not-too-distant future. They include a dormitory for our women employees; a community kitchen and dining hall for the housekeeping colony, where gas might be used for quicker cooking; and open-air amphitheater overlooking the lake; an improved bathing beach to the east below the cabins and cottages; and a medium-sized men's dormitory.

Then before long, could come a good-sized cottage for underprivileged mother and children who otherwise are not reached by the Church. Some truly mission-minded person could make this a fruitful avenue for the gospel of Christian charity in connection with our child-nurture program in Minneapolis. There is a suitable site for such a colony neat the northeast corner of Mount Carmel, just the right distance from the main campus.

The future is in God's hands. He will supply the means wherewith to pay for the present debt on Mount Carmel. He will find men and women ready to support any new venture that is dedicated to unselfish service in His vineyard."

Chapter Four

CAMP DIRECTOR ROY BLOOMQUIST

I had several interviews with Pastor Roy Bloomquist beginning July 25, 2005, which I have summarized. The sentences in quotes are Roy's words, verbatim to me.

Roy began his ministry at Augustana Lutheran Church in Detroit, Michigan after his ordination from Augustana Seminary, in Rock Island, Illinois in 1951. In August of 1955, he and his wife, Marjorie, came to the Lutheran Bible Institute in Minneapolis where he taught Bible. During that year, he had his first contact with Mount Carmel.

After one year he went to teach at the Lutheran Bible Institute in Seattle, Washington. He and Marjorie returned to Minneapolis in 1961 when Roy was asked to replace the retiring Pastor F.W. Klawitter and continue with the daily radio ministry called the *Psalm of Life*.

When Mount Carmel began in 1938, it was an extension of the Lutheran Bible Institute. The Bible teachers from the LBI served as Dean each taking their turn for a week or more during the three months of summer vacation.

In 1965 to 1968, while teaching at the LBI and leading the *Psalm of Life* radio ministry, Roy became the dean of programming at Mount Carmel. Pastor Herbert Malm (Hub) was the business manager. When Malm retired in 1969, Roy became the first director. The new job description combined dean and the business manager into the director position. Roy held this position from 1969 until 1980 when he retired. However, Roy continued with the *Psalm of Life* radio ministry until 1985.

MY GOAL

In the years he and Marge were at Mount Carmel, Roy said, "My goal was simple: I was there to hold Mount Carmel together during its crisis years. First of all, I was not really trained nor equipped to be a camp director. I did my best. I didn't have experience. I didn't have the support I needed."

"When camper registrations dropped off," Roy added, "We had to plan and scrape to survive. At one time, we were down to only four weeks of actual Mount Carmel registered camping, and some of those weeks were not filled. For three summers, we called on Concordia College Language Camp to fill out some of the weeks during the summer. To have that income from Concordia was a matter of financial survival of the camp."

"Their presence can be credited to Mount Carmel's ability to hang on in those years," Roy said, "But, we really had stopped being a Bible Camp. We had lost our focus and our reason for existence...There were people who were beginning to pray for the revival of Mount Carmel. I felt that we should honor the purpose which Dr. Miller pledged for this Bible Camp. Therefore, we should try again to regain the purpose and focus which he had laid out many years ago."

In summary, with the help of these praying people, attendance began to resurge very slowly. The people gained new confidence in the vision and started to come back because people were praying them back.

"But," Roy said, "We received only a few students from the college coming to the camp. I had the very fewest number of staff. It almost baffles me when I think of it," Roy said. "We had sometimes as few as three to five staff, and I had to work them hard. They began to call me the *Gestapo* because I made them work too hard with too many jobs. I couldn't hire staff simply for one task because I didn't have enough registrants to pay the salaries and keep the camp going."

"The budget was a bare minimum, and not only that—but I don't know if you should write this, but..., I will tell you what had happened during the summer for several years. President Bernt Opsal was hoping that there would be some income from the camp to pay the bills at GVLC. God rest Bernt—

a good man trying to do his best at the college—but he would call me on Thursday, after we had taken the evening worship offering. He would say, 'Well, how much do you have?' I would tell him, and then he'd say, 'Send it all here.' Well, I didn't want to do that because I wanted to pay Mount Carmel's bills and have a good credit rating. I tried to protect the registration money. I had to find a way to keep the money hidden for the camp. To tell you the truth, I was trapped! Of course, there was tension between us!"

"Then the people started coming back and the weeks began to fill up." Roy added, "When the times got better, I tried to protect registration money from Bernt. I had to find a way to keep the money hidden. This is because Opsal would have found the money and used it for the debt against the college. Opsal called Mount Carmel his, "ace in the hole."

"Now, whatever he meant by that remark I am not sure, but it was his 'ace in the hole', and he—in other words, he was going to use Mount Carmel whenever he felt there was a time of emergency. That's what it means to me now. Whether he meant that, I don't know! But, like I say, there was constant tension that he wanted to use the money from Mount Carmel for operation of the college."

"I put the money into a bank account in Alexandria, and paid off the note on the sewer, or paid off the bills as they came due. Because of the Language Camp, Mount Carmel not only survived, but we got the sewer project done."

Roy continued, "The sewer system was mandated. Without it, we couldn't have continued to operate. The water district would have closed the camp. They were willing to give us a little extra time, if we needed it. But, we didn't get the district water because we had our own well, and the well was good at that time.

"Bernt never wanted me to take the director position permanently," Roy said. "But nevertheless, after I completed the first year, there wasn't any faculty member, either Wilson Fagerberg, or Backstrom, or whoever was there, none wanted it, so I had to take it. Fagerberg didn't want to touch it, but he wanted to come to Mount Carmel and teach which was good, as he was an excellent teacher."

I Did it All

Roy continued to describe what was happening. "As director and dean and business manager, I did it all. I would direct whatever was the program at that moment. Sometimes, the staff wouldn't empty the garbage. I would look outside and see the garbage wasn't taken down to the dump grounds. I'd stop what I was doing and go down and empty the garbage. Of course, it was due to the fact that we didn't have enough staff."

"My wife, Marge, was the organist and the pianist for the worship services and the programs. She also was in charge of all the special guests, meaning all the Bible teachers for that week and evening speakers. She'd go to town and get supplies that she wanted and then they would just have an afternoon of fellowship. She always invited the guests over to the director's cabin for a little party, usually on Thursday afternoons. She was the hospitality director. But she didn't enter into the business end or the programming. She never worked in the kitchen at meal time."

"I led the worship service every night and the morning chapel meeting sometimes, but I never was the speaker or the Bible teacher in the morning. On Sunday, I led the Sunday Service, but I never preached the sermon. I had the evening speaker for the week be the Sunday morning speaker."

"The fellowship is my biggest good memory of Mount Carmel. And also, the campers' deep appreciation for what Mount Carmel gave them. They all went home happy. If some of them didn't, I didn't know about it." He added, "We always gave them a survey evaluation form to complete on the last day before they left, asking how they felt about Mount Carmel, the food and all their experience. It was always positive. In fact, they were too positive and probably didn't tell the complete truth, because one thing I do regret is that the campers sometimes didn't get enough to eat. We were operating on a tight budget and keeping food costs to an absolute minimum."

"But I tell you Orval, we had terrible financial stress when I was the camp director. However the spiritual experience and the focus on the Bible has been the same. The work of the Spirit is not dependent on how much or how little money you've got. The Spirit of the Lord works!"

46

Roy continued to discuss the workers. "We were hard pressed for workers. We had a hard time getting a cook. The staff did the clean up of the cabins, the dining room and the chapel. We never had an established caretaker. The maintenance work was done by the campers, and the staff."

"I started the idea of having a Memorial Weekend work day to open in the spring with washing the floors and the windows, and making-ready for camp. We asked for volunteers to help us. They responded. Some stayed for several days. Some of them were tough workers. A woman named Helen Savage, and some men such as Stan Hankins from Albert Lea. He is the only guy I ever saw walk up the ladder backwards with a set of shingles on his shoulder. In the fall, on Labor Day weekend, we had the staff close the cabins before they left."

Roy told me that he named the Chapel—Miller, the Dining Hall—Stolee, and the Knock Youth Chapel to honor the originators of Mount Carmel. As the interview came to a close, Roy spoke about his feeling toward Mount Carmel. "I can put it in Marge's words, 'It's the dearest place on earth!' After we left Mount Carmel, whenever we would suggest, 'Let's go for a ride!' she would say, 'Let's go to Mount Carmel.' She loved that place. There was something exciting about it for her, and of course, for me too. The only thing is Mount Carmel was a lot of work."

I asked Roy, "In your opinion, what is the driving force behind Mount Carmel as a ministry and a place for spiritual renewal?"

Roy replied, "It was the founders themselves, men like A. W. Knock and Samuel Miller, who prayed God's blessing on Mount Carmel, that God would use that place mightily. I have heard of a speech by Miller where he expressed himself, that the faculty prayerfully was concerned that Mount Carmel become a continuing spiritual renewal for the people, and it is. It has that same commitment and same dedication. The same expectation has continued from the days when that ground was first committed as a place for the Holy Spirit to work, that commitment continued all these years and it has not wavered in that commitment."

Chapter Five

CAMP DIRECTOR LUTHER LERSETH

LUTHER'S STORY

In the fall of 1978, I accepted the Call to be a Bible teacher at GVLC and to be an assistant football coach. Besides these tasks, I was to be involved with Mount Carmel.

I had close to 20 years experience in the ministry in three northern Canadian churches. I mentioned in my résumé that I was involved in starting three camps in Canada. I had been active in the reorganizing and relocating of a Bible camp in northern Alberta.

My first involvement at Mount Carmel started in the summer of 1979. I came as an assistant director to Rev. Roy Bloomquist who had been the director for several years. I personally took directions from Roy, filling in where needed and doing various tasks. I helped with the maintenance, taught several classes, did most of the beach activities, some advising and counseling, and encouraged the campers and the staff.

I continued in that position the second summer of 1980. In 1981 the Board of Regents along with Dr. Bernt Opsal, decided they wanted a change of direction. They appointed me as the director of Mount Carmel, which lasted four years through 1984. Mount Carmel was heavily in debt. Some say the camp was mortgaged to help the college. However, I was always told it was not mortgaged. I don't know about all the finances that went on behind the scenes between GVLC and Dr. Bernt Opsal, and Mount Carmel. Whatever the case, the running account at the camp was above the line when I was the director and manager.

As director from 1981-1984, my workload increased dramatically. I became responsible for all the programming, hiring of the staff, soliciting volunteers, and scheduling the Bible teachers and preachers. We attempted to bring in strong and capable preachers and speakers. I am thankful for the pastors at GVLC who helped so much in the worship services and in teaching the morning Bible classes.

Pastor Herbert Loddigs was a good standby teacher and friend. He and I spent a lot of time discussing, debating and arguing theological issues. Often we exchanged our thinking for fun to excite the crowd at the camp, and also at the College. I am especially thankful to several pastors—Rev. Homer Larsen, Cedar Falls, IA; Rev. Jim Bjorge, Fargo, ND; and Rev. Carroll Hinderlie, Minneapolis, MN, who gave me their support.

SPRING OF 1981

I remember in the spring of 1981, walking on the grounds of Mount Carmel, stopping and praying, "Lord God, I need someone to come to help, one who knows a lot about technical things. I really need help!" About four or five hours later, Ozzie Sorbel and his wife drove into the camp and said, "I thought I would come and offer my help." He certainly was an answer to my prayer, as well as Delores, his wife.

I made several major operational purchases, as well as directing repairs, and updating facilities and equipment. We improved the kitchen and the appliances. We re-wired the kitchen and put in new convection ovens, a dishwasher and other important kitchen items. We ordered a new walk-in freezer. When the freezer came, it was in a hundred pieces. Fortunately, Ozzie Sorbel, hired as our right hand man, knew how to put it together.

We improved the beach equipment significantly. We put in new docks, swimming decks and worked on the beach itself. We purchased newer cars, pick ups, tractors and lawn equipment. We cut down a lot of dead trees. We painted and re-shingled most of the buildings and updated many cabins. This included putting in new rugs, some new beds and mattresses and new furniture. We updated the speaker system in the chapel. I called in several antique dealers and auctioned the old furniture in the lounge and other old furniture throughout the camp. One dealer bought the whole lot for about $2,500.

The International Harvester tractor and equipment dealer at Alexandria treated us very well. He gave Mount Carmel some tremendous deals in parts and repairs. He made it possible for us to receive major discounts on new equipment and on a small lawn tractor. He was a gracious friend to Mount Carmel.

Some stores and wholesalers of produce treated us very well. Land 0' Lakes gave us milk at a good price. Coca Cola gave us vending machines temporarily so that we could have them for the summer only. Some people came and did work without any charge to the camp. The radio and TV from Alexandria visited Mount Carmel and interviewed us several times, and the newspaper did some catchy articles as well.

I had many great experiences as the director. First of all, having worship services every night, except Saturday, was a tremendous blessing to me and my family. My wife, Jean, and our three teenage sons—Peder, Andrew and Mark spent six summers at Mount Carmel, working many hours, enjoying the camp itself, the staff, visitors and volunteers.

All summer long we were in church six evenings per week, listening to great sermons, wonderful music and happy responsive people and campers. During other times, we had wonderful contact with Christian people. We all felt spiritually uplifted. I hardly had time to watch TV, listen to the radio or read the newspapers. I didn't know anything of the world, except what people told me. Somehow in that arena of life, I was blessed and renewed.

I learned being away from the world had its own rewards. It was a great time for my wife and family. They received many blessings as well. First was the spiritual, second were the people, and the lake, boating, fishing and swimming came after that. The discussions with people, pastors, teachers, campers and staff were wonderful. Working for the Lord full-time plus was very special.

When I was appointed director, I made it clear that I would not allow the schedule of Mount Carmel to destroy my family. I promised that I would be very protective of their rights and life. A few times I had to exercise this promise. Some wondered that my family did not participate in the camp program and did nothing at the camp. By and large, they did very well and helped way beyond what was expected in the camp duties.

Some people were hostile to my changing some scheduling and the staff selection. They asked, "What right does Lerseth have to change the times and the schedule?" Well, there had to be some changes. Some people questioned the camp staff selection process. Of course, we had hard times and various on-going operational problems. Sometimes, the staff had trouble, which we would deal with hands on. By that I mean, some campers would not be happy, but we always tried to make them contented. Once in a while a pastor or teacher on the program would be upset and I tried to comfort them, and help them understand our mission. We always had a nurse to comfort those who were sick. In running a camp, you meet all kinds of people and some with strange needs.

Evaluations of the programs and camp experiences were filled out by every camper at the end of each week. I would read them and make notes. At the end of the season, I would hand them in to Dr. Opsal. He once said to me, "Why do you put the worst on top with red marks?" I answered, "I didn't want you to miss them." There were not many sour ones and in some strange way, I did enjoy them. Most people gave us pretty good grades. Much better than we deserved! Dr. Bernt Opsal was especially good and kind to me and my family. We had a few arguments about running Mount Carmel, but we always ironed them out in peace and quiet. I think we understood each other every well.

As I look back, I think the toughest part of Mount Carmel was my heavy work schedule. I would be working seven days a week from 7:00 a.m. until midnight sometimes, every day all summer. Being in my 40's at that time, I could lie down for five to six hours of sleep and then rise in the newness of life refreshed and ready for the new day. When I think about the length of those days now and the work load, I don't know how I did so many things. I can only give God the credit. And I certainly have no regrets.

Life is up and down like a mountain railroad. There were people who spoke badly about Mount Carmel and tried to undo us. The devil was around at all times. I think we were aware that Satan uses people and things for hurt. Some people tried to cause trouble for different reasons but somehow by the grace of God the problems were quickly dissolved or turned aside.

VANDALISM

There were people who didn't like me or others who were with Mount Carmel. They tried to cause major trouble for us and our operation. We had sabotage on the sewer system and the public works. As an example, someone threw towels to plug up the sewer system that was seven feet or more in depth. One of the lawn mower tractors was also sabotaged. I recall the oil plug was loosened up just enough so it would fall out and ruin the engine. We usually caught the problems before any major damage occurred. We were in a spiritual war, but the Lord was with us.

One fellow said he was going to get at me. I told Dr. Opsal who was sabotaging us—two different men, and he just shook his head. Several times when I was at Mount Carmel alone, I happened to see one of them and realized he was there, hiding and tracking me. I remember praying to God, "I need you now" and the Lord was there and gave me the protection I needed. We had a job to do. We had a purpose and a mission, and I was determined to get it done.

I was often asked how we made so many improvements and yet we tried to run the camp in the black financially. I always prayed for guidance, used common sense and called on the people to support Mount Carmel, pointing out the benefits and blessings of our camp. I was amazed how people responded. It was always beyond expectation. Even to this day, people ask me about Mount Carmel, our food and programming.

We hired the best cooks we could get and could afford. But, we were often short of money for wages and staples. However, after improving the kitchen and food source, many people thought our simple meals at Mount Carmel were delightful. One of the important things was to ensure that people didn't think they would starve before the next meal. But, we had nothing to spare.

We also made a great attempt to improve the music program. We invited real good music people from GVLC and they did a bang-up job. Many campers made great comments about the music and I was very proud of the music efforts at Mount Carmel. The young people really put themselves out for the camp and the glory of God. I often said to the music people, "Let's make it great for the people who came to Mount Carmel and they did."

I was so happy and thankful for the staff that once in awhile, I took over half of the staff in to town for a pizza night. Later on the GVLC financial staff asked me, "What are these occasional $100 miscellaneous items?" I often answered, "As little as we pay these students and as hard as we work them, I wouldn't complain." I added "If it's a problem, take it out of my wages." They never did. I made an effort to keep everyone happy and joyful I reminded them, "What a privilege to work for the Lord this way and be at Mount Carmel." I felt that way and I believe they did as well.

SPIRIT OF THE CAMP

When I became director, my hopes and goals were simply to do the work of God and be faithful to the task set before us. The goal was to work and serve the plan of salvation through Jesus Christ the Lord. That was our purpose!

Jean, my wife, always felt Mount Carmel was a great experience for us. She was especially gifted in dealing with people. She was very helpful, loving, caring, and able to handle her place at the camp. She had a spirit of openness and spoke clearly and plainly to people. She paid special attention to those who felt lonely and maybe left out. Jean was happy and thankful for the Mount Carmel experience we had together.

The great experiences, the programs, the people, the spiritual times, the location on Lake Carlos, the hard work, and the rewards and the blessings were unbelievable to say the least. Some people recognized our efforts, others didn't and some didn't care. But our relationship with God and our inner reward was great.

I was thankful for the times I could preach and teach the Bible. Sometimes pastors couldn't get to Mount Carmel on time and I would fill in for them. The fellowship and the discussion times were special when we talked about our faith and action as Christian people. I remember sitting late at night in the swing chair outside our cabin, down on the west end of the camp. I would meditate and spend time alone with the Lord, looking across the lake at the blinking lights and haze of light from Alexandria. Those were the special moments. Once in awhile someone would see me and come and talk with me. It was in those late night contacts, I felt so close to God and also in the early morning.

When the time came for us to say our goodbyes, I pushed for Pastor Johan Hinderlie to come as the new director of the camp. I thought he would do a good job. I also felt it was important that the new director have only the one job as director of the camp, so that a good job could be done.

We haven't been back very often or too long. We have seen pictures of the new buildings and rejoice that Mount Carmel continues to do so well. For Mount Carmel, I thank God and all that went with it. It was great to be numbered among the people who lived and worked for the Lord Jesus Christ in that holy place.

Chapter Six

CAMP DIRECTOR JOHAN HINDERLIE

A VISION FOR GOD'S WORK

I first heard about Mount Carmel in 1966 from my friend Paul Loddigs when I was a college sophomore working as summer staff at a Bible Camp in Minnesota. His dad, Herb, was our Bible teacher and Paul would take me for rides in his boat. We had been friends for years, but this summer made that relationship very strong. One of the days that we were together, Paul and I were talking about Holden Village and how important its ministry had been to me. Paul then told me about Mount Carmel. His voice changed a little becoming quite serious and deep and I could see something peaceful in his eyes. He said, "Mount Carmel; that is the most beautiful place I have ever been."

Paul's comments were so compelling. It was a tone I was not used to hearing since he was normally not that serious. But it convicted me and the impression it left on me still affects me as I think about this place and its power for our Lord.

Another friend who was a frequent teacher over the years was Pastor Bill Hulme, a professor of Pastoral Care at Luther Seminary in St. Paul. I was sitting with a group of people one day listening to Bill teach and he made this comment about Mount Carmel. "Mount Carmel is the closest thing to heaven of any place I have ever been on earth."

There are many others whose voices for the value of this ministry have touched me over the years. But all of them have given me the sense that God had something special in mind for the people who came to this place of beauty. In my years of ministry here, I have sought to be sensitive to the voice of our Lord so that I do not get in the way of what God wants to do here.

My First Contact

I contacted Luther Lerseth in April of 1984 about bringing a group of young people from my church in Wisconsin to Mount Carmel for a week when Herb Loddigs and my dad, Carroll Hinderlie were teaching and preaching. Lerseth told me he had taken a new Call back to a church in Canada, saying, "Maybe you should have this job at Mount Carmel." The effect of his off-the-cuff suggestion opened my mind to an idea that Sonja and I believed our Heavenly Father wanted for us. We had prayed about this for several years. The prayer was that some day we might be able to do a ministry similar to what we had experienced at Holden Village. We had even written down a plan of action and our hope for such a position.

When Lerseth made his comment, I thought maybe it was just another opportunity for Bible Camp work. I had applied to be the director of a Bible Camp in southern Wisconsin and had been turned down. When I made a phone call to the Golden Valley Lutheran College, which owned Mount Carmel, I knew very little about Mount Carmel except that it was in Minnesota.

But I told Herb Loddigs about Lerseth's suggestion. He was delighted and then he said, "How can we figure out a way to make the president of the college think it was his idea?" I had to leave that to Herb. The President, Pastor Bernt Opsal, told me they were not interviewing for a director. But, at the same time he left open a door for an on-going conversation. He later called and said, "I have been thinking about your phone call to me, and maybe the position would include some other possibilities." He asked, "How are you at public relations and marketing and what other talents do you have?" The president arranged for a meeting in July. We talked about a number of responsibilities at the college. He had a plan for me. Herb had succeeded. And of course the Holy Spirit helped as well.

CALL TO GOLDEN VALLEY LUTHERAN COLLEGE

In August, while I was in New York, I received a Letter of Call to a position in the college, and I accepted it. Pastor Alf Romstad, the pastor of Opsal's church, and a good friend of mine had died and I came for his funeral on Labor Day weekend. After the funeral, Opsal drove me to Mount Carmel, which was my first experience there.

My Call wasn't to Mount Carmel. Rather it was to GVLC in church relations, with support to the staff and students. The college did not have a campus pastor and that position became a part of my responsibility. Mount Carmel was a principle part of my job. I inherited it. I promoted Mount Carmel as part of my duties that fall and winter.

I arrived at Golden Valley Lutheran College in October of 1984. Shortly after I arrived, I began contacting faculty for the summer program. My first summer as the director at Mount Carmel would be in 1985. I looked over the list of names of teachers and preachers who had come here in past summers and did a lot of calling and talking. I was surprised how long it took me. I calculated about 25 days of work to get all the resource people contacted, dates and messages arranged and then to produce the brochure. And after this came the job of finding summer staff.

Fortunately the college had a wonderful supply of creative and motivated Christian youth who were willing to work. And there were some great people who came to see me from previous summers.

One of these was Mark Kindem. This giant man stopped in my office one day and looked around at my room and then stared at me and said, "I'm here to work. I love Mount Carmel. When can I begin?" He was graduating from college in the spring and came right away in May. Mark lived on our site for two winters starting that fall. He became a tremendous friend and a big brother to my sons.

Another funny conversation came from an Ethiopian named Ale Tulu. He was a student at the college. And my conversation with him was about his history. He said, "I know you are looking for summer staff. Many are from Norwegian background. Would you consider hiring me? You know I am Norwegian. But I come from the southern part of Norway where we get more sun." Ale (pronounced Ah-lee) served as a summer staff for seven years and he and his wife were married here. His story deserves its own book.

God knew the people He wanted to bring to Mount Carmel.

I came to see from many of these experiences that it was truly God's property and His ministry. And He was the one who had the plans for it with the people. I had to learn to listen to Him. But what happened next no one was prepared for at all.

GOLDEN VALLEY LUTHERAN COLLEGE CLOSED

In late April of 1985, the news broke that Golden Valley Lutheran College would be closing. The Board of Trustees for the college borrowed $300,000 from the American Lutheran Church to pay the bills in the month of May so that the students could finish out the school year and graduate. The distress on campus was huge. We all hoped and prayed there could be some way to change the outcome. But freshman students who came for a weekend orientation were met by admissions counselors from Augsburg College in Minneapolis. It was a very sad time. Just about everyone on the staff and faculty was asked to leave.

When the college closed, I was one of the few people on the payroll who did not depend on students for my salary. One of the reasons was the *Psalm of Life* radio ministry.

Pastor Roy Bloomquist, a former director of Mount Carmel, had served as the radio preacher for the *Psalm of Life* for many years. Its first preacher and founder in 1945 was Pastor Ernie Klawitter. The fifteen minute program started out as a live broadcast over WCAL—of St. Olaf College in Northfield, MN, every weekday morning from a location on the campus of the Lutheran Bible Institute in Minneapolis. By 1985 recorded messages in a studio on the Golden Valley campus were sent to all the stations that broadcast our program. But Roy chose to retire in February. President Opsal asked me if I could take his position over until they found a full-time preacher. So I began preaching on the *Psalm of Life* radio ministry that spring in 1985, and I retained the position as the radio pastor for 15 years until we ended the radio ministry in 2000. So when the college closed, my two main responsibilities were Mount Carmel and the *Psalm of Life*.

FIRST SUMMER

About 700 people came that summer to Mount Carmel. We cancelled one week because we didn't get enough registrations. We were trying to build a positive outlook about the future, although everyone was feeling depressed with the closing of the college.

About the only thing that I was ready to change the first summer was the Sunday morning preacher. Previous years the evening preacher would preach on Sunday mornings but I knew I needed to have a way to share my convictions and my vision with the people. So I started preaching on Sundays and have been the Sunday morning preacher ever since.

I also had the challenge of keeping the *Psalm of Life* broadcasts going in the summer. I would drive down to Minneapolis regularly to do my radio program. Twice I was able to use the recording studio of one of the radio stations in Alexandria. This responsibility was a lot more challenging than I had expected.

MOUNT CARMEL DEBT

Another thing I wanted to do to build confidence was to schedule a meeting each week with any guests who wanted to come to talk about the college's closing and what this might mean for the ministry at Mount Carmel. These also gave me a chance to listen to the concerns that these old friends of Mount Carmel might have.

At one of these meetings, a guest came up and asked, "How about this debt that's borrowed against Mount Carmel?"

I said, "What debt? I didn't know there was a debt." He said, "Yes, there is a debt on Mount Carmel, and it's for $480,000." I said, "I don't know anything about this." He continued, "Yes sir, it's with a bank in Minneapolis."

A few days later, he said to me, "You should go check the records at Douglas County. That's where I found out the debt." So I went to the Register of Deeds, and I discovered an additional debt of $300,000, which was a loan from the American Lutheran Church. Surprising to me, there was a total of about $800,000 worth of obligations on the land at Mount Carmel.

After discovering the information about the two major loans against the Mount Carmel property, people each week said farewell with a feeling of tremendous disappointment. We had a lot of people who said, "The situation seems hopeless. Not only do we have old buildings and a small number of people participating, but we also are in debt $800,000."

MOUNT CARMEL...OUR FIRST YEAR

The year of 1986 was terribly difficult for us at Mount Carmel because we didn't have the college from which to recruit staff or faculty. Very few people were willing to send in any money to support the college, Mount Carmel or even the *Psalm of Life* (we had no money to pay salaries in January of '86). Sonja and I were expected to find our own way, since the board of trustees for the college and LBI was focused on its sale. On the bright side, we had Mark Kindem living on the property which helped my morale since he was problem solver and could fix anything. Then when I became the interim president of LBI, and the defunct GVLC, I arranged for Sonja to become the summer director.

She effectively took over my job and worked at developing the summer program. She put together a plan of action so that we moved from 700 guests in 1985 to 1600 guests in 1986. It seemed unbelievable that our attendance more than doubled in just one year. It was a significant change with several new weekend groups, and lots of other new people. Remember that these were the old cabins that were basically unimproved, which had no hot water, just cold water. These were very simple places, nothing fancy about them at all. We did have a good cook who was a lot of fun who did a fantastic job in the kitchen, but unfortunately there just wasn't a lot of money, so we were struggling all year with costs.

We did generate enough income with money left over, showing enough improvement that the chairman of the board of the Lutheran Bible Institute had confidence to believe the Mount Carmel program could continue. The Rev. Howard Sortland had taken over as the chairman of the board of trustees. Howard worked with the college's financial advisor on ideas and possibilities for the future. Howard developed creative plans for the ministry. He was a key to the survival of the ministry.

FROM STEERING COMMITTEE TO MOUNT CARMEL MINISTRIES

Sortland helped put together a plan whereby we could create a steering committee to plan the future of Mount Carmel. At a meeting set for August 9, 1986, a group of about 60 friends met at Mount Carmel and selected the following people to help shape Mount Carmel. These people were Helen Savage, Norm Anderson, Ernie Bakken, Jim Nelson, Charles Blastervold, Linda Simpson, Wally Ness, Neal Eriksmoen and Irene Myhro.

One of the first things this committee did was to help raise money from a group of friends to pay off the debt on the property. The Golden Valley Bank had not been paid anything on its loan for 6 years and they wanted something done or they would have to take action for a takeover of the property.

Given the urgency of the demand, several members of the steering committee came to Sonja and me, and said, "We need to raise money to pay off the debt on Mount Carmel." In talking over all the options, we figured that if we got in around $700,000, we could pay off the Golden Valley Bank debt and the American Lutheran Church. We needed a letter and we wrote one asking friends to consider a $1000 gift or more. We hoped we could take in the $700,000.

In all we raised $155,000 in cash. People were encouraged and contributed thousands of dollars. But $155,000 was still a long way from the $700,000 that we wanted and needed.

We continued to send out new information and requests to people. There was encouragement because the successful summer program showed there were new signs of life. People felt good about the things they saw at Mount Carmel.

Then the steering committee decided to create a not for profit organization. It created its own Board of Directors from the steering committee and became a legal corporation. It established a 501(c) 3, so Mount Carmel could receive the donations as benevolence. All the checks that came in were deposited into the newly formed Mount Carmel Ministries Corporation. It was called Mount Carmel Ministries because our two key ministries were the site, Mount Carmel, and our outreach tool, the *Psalm of Life* radio ministry.

Sonja had become the president of the Mount Carmel Ministries organization. I was the interim president of LBI and the preacher for the *Psalm of Life*. The members of the Board met once a month to evaluate the financial status of Mount Carmel. The new Board governed the decisions regarding the money that was received from any source.

FINANCIAL CRISIS

Late in the fall of 1986, the Board had to decide whether to send the $155,000 back to the donors, or try to solve the financial problem of the debt on the campus with less money than needed. This was a very difficult moment for the Board. Every meeting was spent praying and planning. Sonja and Chuck Blastervold went to the Golden Valley Bank to talk. The bank officials said they would forgive the interest on the loan—about $60,000. But, they also said, "We will not give you a mortgage on the property as long as the American Lutheran Church has a $300,000 second mortgage claim against it." This now became a very difficult problem.

So Chuck and Sonja went to talk to leaders of the ALC. And they asked the Rev. T. Arnold Thompson to also go with them to the ALC headquarters in downtown Minneapolis. Arnie was a persuasive person. And he knew his way around the ALC organization having been its Director for American Missions for years. He persuaded some of the leaders that if Mount Carmel could survive for ten years they should forgive the $300,000 loan. This made it possible for the holder of the first mortgage, which was the Golden Valley Bank, to have a clear title. We now believed we could continue the operation and make it work.

What Arnie was able to get from the ALC was a miracle. In summary, they said: We will forgive the loan if you are successful in operating the ministry for ten years. All we had to do was to be successful for ten years. If they had demanded payment of the $300,000 at that time, Mount Carmel would not be here today. In the event that a sale was made of the land, the ALC made a claim that they would stand second in line for payment after the Golden Valley Bank.

When the Board of Trustees of the ALC made the decision and promise to forgo the interest and the loan, the bank could then consider a loan on the basis of the $420,000 that the bank was owed. The fact is in 1980, GVLC borrowed this money for its operations using Mount Carmel as collateral for the loan. Sonja had been working with a vice-president at the bank to see what kind of terms we could achieve.

With this assurance, the Mount Carmel Board chose not to send the donated money back, but rather to put the money into a savings account to be used for a down payment on a new mortgage at a later date.

In January of 1987, during the annual meeting for the LBI, 71 voting members of LBI voted unanimously to allow Mount Carmel Ministries to take over the $780,000 debt of Mount Carmel. Now the way was clear to create a new loan to pay off the bank portion of the debt on the Mount Carmel property. The Mount Carmel Ministries Corporation had $155,000 in its savings account to initiate payments for the new mortgage on the property.

All the money given to save Mount Carmel was accounted for by the new Board. None of the new money went to the College. Previously the LBI had been responsible for the fiscal supervision of the ministry.

On the 17th of March, 1987, St. Patrick's Day, the transfer of the property, and the debt from LBI to Mount Carmel took place. A new loan was created and $75,000 of the money raised from donations was paid against the debt. A $345,000 loan was established at nine percent interest with the Golden Valley Bank. We were required to pay interest only for the next five years.

THE PROCLAIMERS

In 1987 we started the Proclaimers, which was vital for our ministry. We contracted for financial guidance and services with a consultant named Dick Sayther. He suggested we needed a giving club that would support this ministry. We needed a name and a plan. He mentioned the word proclamation, and said, "We need something that identifies why you do what you do. I think you do ministry because you are Proclaimers. You have something to tell the world."

The idea of proclamation and Proclaimers is found in the Bible— Matthew 4:23, NRSV, where it says, "*Jesus came proclaiming the Kingdom of God.*" We used the image that anyone who comes to Mount Carmel is renewed in Christ with a message to proclaim. The Proclaimers are renewed people, who have a message from Jesus to share with the world. The Proclaimers donated about $70,000 that first year. And over five million dollars have come from these loyal supporters since that time.

The Proclaimers are important for several reasons. Basically, the Proclaimers are the owners of the ministry. They are the people who actually elect the Board of Trustees and provide the basis for the ministry. The Proclaimers know where their money will be spent and the directors of the ministry share their commitments for Mount Carmel.

The legal entitlement of being a Proclaimer is written into our constitution and the bylaws, as is the term Proclaimers. To be a Proclaimer means a person who contributes a set amount of money each year and participates in the ministry. This gives the person the right to participate in the election of the Board of the Corporation.

The By-laws determine that any new Board member must be chosen from current Proclaimers by a nominating committee made up of the Chair of the Board, the Executive Director and one Proclaimer not on the Board. New Board nominations have to be approved by the current Board and then the nominees are elected by the Proclaimers as a whole with a written ballot sent to all Proclaimers. No write in candidates are allowed.

50ᵀᴴ Anniversary

The year 1988—the 50th anniversary—seems to be one of the turning points in the story of Mount Carmel. Many people did a lot of work getting ready for that celebration. We set aside about $25,000 renewal and to celebrate the future. We added showers and bathrooms to six cabins, 1, 21, 22, 23, 24, 26. Until then, we had only outdoor shower houses. We wanted to fix up those cabins as a sign that we were moving in a new direction with the ministry.

We also created the Jubilee Trail, the walking trail that leads into the woods near the place where the boats are stored. It was the 50th year and a Jubilee moment. Right after the 50th anniversary, we implemented Dick Sayther's idea called the Stepping Stone, which would "step down the payments" against the debt of the campus. The Stepping Stone plan raised about $100,000 in cash against the debt on the property from 1989 through the summer of 1992. We still owed about $250,000 on the loan and we were paying the interest and some money on the principle.

In the fall of 1988, we began working with a master planner consultant to put together a plan for Mount Carmel's future. We brought him in to review the property, and begin to create a master plan.

First Master Plan

The first Master Plan encouraged reviewing our mission and purpose. A task force process called for a plan of action to fully develop the property with specific buildings to be replaced and the grounds enhanced. We drew up a schematic of the grounds and projected new buildings. We looked at every possible opportunity with dreams and goals for the land and the ministry. Specifically involved in those discussions was what to do to rebuild or replace the dining hall that had major structural problems. The foundation was rotting, and the walls could potentially buckle with a heavy snow.

From 1989 through 1991 a process of conversation about that dining hall developed. In 1991, we hired an architect—Lloyd Jafvert to help us with a concept. He came up with a drawing that we presented to the constituency as a plan for the new dining hall. In the summer of 1992, two members of our Board of Trustees, Bernie Youngquist and Neil Eriksmoen, met every week with guests to explain the need for this new plan and ministry. The goal was to build the new dining hall and to move into a winterized program. Of course, money again was an issue.

CHALLENGE TO PAY OFF THE DEBT

In the summer of 1992, Dr. Courtland Agre had an inspiration which I believe was from the Holy Spirit. This event totally changed the course of action in Mount Carmel.

Courtland had called me several times about the debt with the bank, which seemed to bother him to no end. He informed me that he even had been to visit officers at the bank.

I went with him one time to the Golden Valley Bank. We went in to visit the bank president and Court basically said, "I will write you a check today if you will discount the loan," and he said "No. That's not in our interest because we are getting payments on the interest of the debt all the time." But Courtland's particular passion was used by God into enabling Mount Carmel to be debt free.

Dr. Courtland Agre had a meaningful history with Mount Carmel through his friends at Lutheran Bible Institute. He knew some of the teachers and pastors from the days of his youth. He had been up to Mount Carmel with his family when he was younger. His kids had been there with him. So he loved Mount Carmel.

He was a brilliant man who had been professor of chemistry, first at St. Olaf, and then at Augsburg College until he retired. He and Ellen are the parents of several children including Dr. Peter Agre who was awarded the Nobel Prize for Chemistry. In his retirement, Courtland would come up and work as a volunteer. He would paint cabins and trim shrubs. He just had a very strong passion for the ministry and the sacredness of this place. He knew some of our buildings were in bad shape because wearing his old white laboratory coat, he had been scraping old paint and repainting cabin after cabin. Courtland did not like the fact that we were in debt and believed it was a major hindrance for ministry.

After the Sunday morning worship service on July 22, he and I were standing in the front of Miller Chapel off to the side near one of the little rooms for prayer. He seemed to be especially nervous. He had been inspired with the singing and sermon and the whole worship service. He said to me, "I wanted to stand up and make a challenge to the people during the Sunday morning service."

I said, "What did you want to do?"

He said, "My wife and I want to give a gift. We want to make a challenge for everybody who is here to meet that gift."

His belief was if he and his wife would give so much money, then other people will also give the same. His challenge was that he would give $35,000. Anybody who was a guest that week would be challenged together to match his offer, but they had to give it in cash before the end of the year.

In addition, he said, "We'll also give an additional $15,000 which will bring the gift up to $50,000 if the people who are here together will give a total of $70,000. This will give us a grand total of $120,000 in cash. But, we have to receive all the pledges in one week."

I said, "Well, that's going to be kind of hard to do in one week." To myself I thought, "the wealthier supporters of Mount Carmel are not here this week." But out loud I said, "Let's do it." I called the Chairman of the Board, and told him what was going on and that Courtland would make his challenge on Tuesday night. 'I think you should come down and hear it, 'I told him so he drove down from his home and listened.

After the evening meal, Courtland invited all of us from dinner into that little lounge area of the old dining hall by the stone fireplace. There we had the meeting. Dr. Agre stood up to speak.

Courtland in summary made the challenge for the people gathered to match the gift he and his wife would give. And then he added this shocker!

"But," he said, "If you don't meet it, we will give nothing."

I remember that! He said, "Nothing!" And, I thought, 'wow, how could he be so severe?' It was all or nothing! Well of course, that idea got people thinking and talking and wondering. People went with looks of surprise, and maybe bewilderment, and some with questions on their faces. They began to try to figure out what they could give in terms of a gift. They could make a pledge that week, but it had to be paid in cash by the end of the year. That was firm!

The word spread quickly. People heard about this challenge. There were people coming from out of the local area, who were interested, too. But Courtland limited the challenge to those who were guests at Mount Carmel that week. By Thursday we had raised about $40,000, so we were assured of their gift of $35,000.

But during the week Courtland confided to me, "Okay, we've done so well, we'll roll the offer over into next week and see what you can do with those guests." He told me that so that I would relax because I will admit I was anxious. That Sunday, I could tell the motivation and excitement were high as we were sure we were going to reach the $70,000 goal. Even the staff members came up with $3500 in cash commitments. To see what they did was really exciting. The whole feeling had a momentum for people wanting to give.

A guest from Alexandria, who didn't want his identity known at that time, came to me on the next Tuesday and said, "My wife and I are going to give $6,000 toward this appeal tonight."

I said to him, "Why don't you hold your money, because I think we are going to meet the goal and maybe we could start another challenge after this one is done, and get the whole debt taken care of." On Thursday night he came back to the chapel, and I said, "Well, what did you two decide?"

He said, "We changed our minds. Instead of giving $6,000, we are giving $25,000." Another shock! Now we could start the second phase of the challenge. I called two other people who had indicated they would donate. One of them gave $15,000 and another gave $10,000, so we had another $50,000. The three major donors were Don and Donna Hustad from Alexandria, and Marlin and Peggy Johnson from Bismarck, North Dakota, and Norman and Jan Anderson from Cumberland, Wisconsin. At first they did not want to be known as the major donors. But after all these years they need to be credited because the camp turned around financially after that summer. It was because of challenge of Dr. Agre and his wife Ellen, these other three major donations and the generosity of many others as well including the Proclaimers that Mount Carmel survived and has prospered.

One of the most meaningful of the gifts I received during this time came from a high school boy living in Alexandria who played the piano for us for some of our services. He made a personal pledge of $100 and I wept since I knew how little money he had. But that was the spirit that had overcome Mount Carmel. Everyone wanted to do what they could.

In the next 20 days, I wrote letters to all the people on our mailing list. The letters said, "We have just raised $120,000. We now have another $50,000 challenge. If we could get another $70,000, we will have $240,000 and we will pay off our debt," and we did. We did! We made it. There was a deadline. Those three men and their wives who gave the $25,000, the $15,000 and the $10,000 each had a deadline as well and everyone met the deadline and that's how the original debt was paid.

When we got the news that all the pledges were in and we would get the challenges met, one of the boys who was at Mount Carmel went running from the chapel to the dining hall yelling out, "We did it; we did it."

DINING HALL PLANNED AND THE SLEEPING WING SURPRISE

When we built the new dining hall which we call the Lodge, we had major gifts from some of these same people. We had major gifts in the amounts of $20,000, $30,000, $50,000 and $100,000. But the key to our success has always been the thousands that have come in from the many smaller gifts. But the key is that people who give share a vision with the outcome of the ministry that the gifts will accomplish.

Early in the summer of 1996, the Board of Trustees was preparing for the demolition of the old dining hall and building of the new one beginning on Labor Day. At that time, two brothers, John and Jim Bjorge came with a challenge to the Board. They said we should consider building the wing with the 10 bedrooms at the same time. We expected the 10 sleeping rooms to cost about $300,000, but of course it ended up costing us much more than that. Yet, the plan worked.

John and Jim came to the guests every week and shared their challenge. Several friends caught the vision and pledged $30,000 for one bedroom. One church in Edina had sold its property and gave a room to the Lodge. Many friends donated money in honor of Kay and Dick Hoffland as well as Marva Dawn and rooms were created with these gifts The money continued to come, and the dining hall was finished in 1997 with the sleeping rooms in 1998.

During this time, two families gave us low interest loans totaling $50,000 to help us with our financial challenge. And then they began to forgive their claim.

It is always amazing to me about Mount Carmel. I have been so accustomed to things happening in funny ways that I can never predict how the Lord will work next in the lives of His people.

UNUSUAL HELP

During the first five years of our ministry we had major gifts from a variety of people who were not Lutherans. One Methodist couple gave us $10,000 in the late 80's; a Pentecostal couple paved the main road from the entrance all the way down to the Youth Chapel. And it was a Roman Catholic couple that kept the place running on the shoestring of money that we could afford in the 90's.

Jerry Lang came to work with us in 1990 and served here until the end of the decade. With his wife Jan, they did everything to keep the buildings operational as well as all our equipment. Jan volunteered all during this time. Their loyalty was amazing. One of the most noticeable benefits Jerry gave our ministry was the installation of a bathroom in the old Dining Hall. He had to crawl all the way under the building to do this. But it was definitely a great blessing to all of us. In some ways, Jerry saved Mount Carmel for all of us. Even after the debt was paid off in 1992, we still struggled financially, yet he did so many things because he was able and creative. We dedicated cabin # 2 in honor of both Jerry and his wife, Jan. They did so much for Mount Carmel. No one will ever know how much they did to enable the camp to survive and maintain a ministry.

In 1999, after Jerry retired, the Board hired Marv Nysetvold to serve as the onsite manager of Mount Carmel. Marv and his wife Theresa had worked on the summer staff and were involved in the ministry here every summer with their family. Marv's job as the Assistant Director was to oversee the new Lodge making sure that it was ready for use by weekend guests. In order to do this effectively, he and his family lived on the site for a little over four years. He built up the great reputation our ministry has for winter retreat groups handling them himself or hiring help to serve in his absence.

Marv also was responsible for hiring the staff who would help with the operations. He hired Verney Klemm, our Buildings and Grounds director, as well as all the summer staff. And he worked with a number of staff who served on a limited basis for a year at a time as winter retreat host or hostess. Jill Manlove, who serves this role full time now, was hired by Marv.

Marv's love for this place was key to his value for our winter ministry having led the way here as our first year-round resident in years.

M&M Appeal

When the Dining Hall and Sleeping Wing project was completed we still owed a little over 1 Million dollars for the construction. We were able to get a loan from Lutheran Brotherhood. But it was still too big of a debt for us.

So in the winter of 1999, several people got together to talk about a way to get the debt paid off completely. Kay Hoffland came up with the idea of the appeal, calling it the Million in the Millennium Appeal or the "M&M" appeal. She teamed up with several others, including Don Waldeland, to create a fun way to raise money. Kay wanted every person to give one dollar for each year of his or her life and then to add a zero or two to the total. One 90 year old friend gave us $9000.00. Kids would give their age. Some just gave a random sum. People got the excitement. One Sunday morning the regular worshippers gave $65,000 in cash gifts for the appeal. It was lots of fun and very stimulating for all of us to see how God was keeping the fire of Mount Carmel alive in the spirit of the giving for this ministry.

It was a great success. We launched the idea in the fall of 1999 and all of 2000 and during this time we raised about $750,000 in cash. It did not leave us debt free but we paid the debt down to about the amount of $250,000.

Psalm of Life and Paul Loddigs

During the first fifteen years of my ministry, I preached on the radio as the *Psalm of Life* pastor. 1985-86 was very challenging for me with all the changes at Mount Carmel and then my new work as a radio preacher. It is tough to preach into a microphone with the same kind of enthusiasm and zeal that you get from a congregation.

Our producer for the broadcasts was Paul Loddigs. He got involved due to his interest in video and audio work. I did not have much money to pay him when we started so I would give him equipment from the college office in lieu of cash. He got tape recorders and tables from the college. This worked for awhile. When I began working full time at Mount Carmel in 1987 with responsibility for both the radio and the camping ministry, we had some money we could budget for the programs.

Our biggest challenge over the years was keeping our radio broadcast times consistent. Our hardest hits came from WCAL in Northfield since it was the station that had the widest broadcast and when it was sold to the University of Minnesota in 1991, our ministry had to change.

Paul and I would work hard to find ways to resolve the problems with our stations. We went to a weekly program which we called, "A Time for Hope" over some of the stations when we could not afford the weekday ministry. But it seemed to be a losing battle.

We began using our online ministry at dailytext.com with some of our broadcasts since this was free to us but people had to tune in which was less common in those days. Toward the end our ministry of the *Psalm of Life*, it was totally dedicated to using the web page as our ministry outlet. But even this we could no longer afford after 2000.

Paul and I had many wonderful ideas with the program. Early on we even went on a tour to some of the towns where the program was being broadcast and once did some programs as far away as Jamestown, NY.

Paul was a resourceful and generous person whose many ideas for programs and marketing kept us alive for longer than we should have hoped. But it finally came to an end. And this part of the Mount Carmel story is sad. For not only did the program die, but my friend Paul also died on December 25 in 2005. I am thankful for the privilege I had to work with him and to be called his friend. Together we shared many adventures as children of unusual earthly dads and as children of an even more unusual Heavenly Dad.

DAILY TEXTS

The most important personal part of my ministry has been my work with the *Daily Texts*. When I graduated from seminary I was asked by the teachers who reviewed me and approved me for ordination if I had a devotional life. I told them I did not. Their concern was how I could be a shepherd to my flock if I did not have a regular conversation with the Good Shepherd. Well, nothing much had changed until my wife and I met Ingrid Trobisch.

Ingrid taught Sonja and me how to pray together using the *Daily Texts* and a prayer form that she and Walter had adapted from Martin Luther. They asked four questions of the verses that they would read starting with the words, thank, regret, prayer and plan. Later a friend at Mount Carmel suggested that we change the word "prayer" to "intercession" to create the word T.R.I.P.

The benefit of learning how to pray Scripture together surprised me. It resulted in some very powerful outcomes.

The first was that Sonja and I began to experience an intimacy in our life we had never known before. The second outcome was that I learned to practice giving thanks as a normal way to respond to what God does for me daily as revealed in the Bible. The third surprise in this process was that the stronghold of codependency that was ruining my life was broken. It took 13 months of journaling our prayers but the Devil's influence over me was broken and I was free. Jesus told us:

> *If you journal and surround yourself with my words, you will be my follower, and you will know what it is to be real, and this reality will make you free.*
>
> (John 8:31-36, NRSV)

What I got from this time of praying is freedom. I am free.

I still have these regular conversations with my Lord and they keep changing me as I spend time with Him. If any of you who are reading this want to learn more about how you can get free and converse with the Lord, please contact me. It takes time and it takes honesty but the change will come. God's Word works!

One of the couples whose lives were changed like ours are David and Cheryl Doely. They were pastors in Iowa in the late 90's and we would work on couple retreats together along with about 7 other couples. When Cheryl began to work for the NE Iowa Synod of the ELCA, she told me they wanted to buy enough *Daily Texts* for all their pastors and others in their synod. With their commitment in1996 we created the first Mount Carmel version of the *Daily Texts*.

Since then we have produced over 200,000 books. These little devotionals are changing lives all over the world. We have sent as many as 7000 to soldiers in Iraq in one year. We have had wonderful "textimonials" from people who use the book. The *Daily Texts* is the book we use every day at Mount Carmel to keep our lives connected to the living God.

SECOND MASTER PLAN

The Board undertook a second Master Plan in the fall of 2003. A great deal of time and conversation went into this work. The outcome of all this evaluation was to recommend a 5 Million Dollar capital campaign called "Building Blessings."

The goal of this campaign was to produce the kind of facilities at Mount Carmel that would make our teaching and preaching ministry stronger for the summer and expand our service in the winter months. One of the goals for the winter was to create an educational center where young people could get biblical training for ministry. The idea of a ministry training center, or "MTC", had been discussed over the years but now it became a value for which we were ready to pledge time and dollars.

THE NEW CABINS

The first priority of "Building Blessings" was for cabins. As age has taken its toll on all of the buildings, the Board has looked for ways to rebuild or renovate the cabins. Summer guests had indicated that they preferred cabins to lodge rooms. And it was discussed that cabins could be used to house students in the winter as the "MTC" is developed as a teaching center for college aged youth.

Some of the housekeeping cabins were moved to the west end of the campus. New cabins were built in the space left behind. The first of those was built in 2005 and was named after Hans Nielson Hauge, the reformer who brought revival to the Norwegians. This first new cabin painted blue was dedicated and named on August 12, 2006. On the same Proclaimer Weekend of August 12, the Board approved the construction of two more cabins located near the Hauge cabin. These new housekeeping cabins are similar in design with a few minor changes. They are named in honor of Jacob Spener and Grundtvig, reformers in Germany and Denmark and were dedicated in the summer of 2007 when the donors for them were present.

LEARNING CENTER AND CHAPEL

The new Learning Center and Chapel began to rise from the old chapel's foundation on October 8th, 2007 after it was demolished. It was a difficult day for all of us to witness the removal of that beloved building. Every possible feeling and memory that one can imagine filled our hearts as the huge claws from the yellow steel back hoe took its first bite. Thousands of people had seen their spiritual lives renewed and refreshed sitting in that old building. Hundreds had received spiritual growth and enrichment by the ministry that occurred in Miller Chapel over the past seven decades.

The Board and leaders of Mount Carmel knew several years ago that the building would require extensive structural repair or replacement. Cost wise, the Board at first decided to repair and refurbish the building. However, further investigation by structural engineers showed that too much money would be needed to meet the new standards required. After prayer, conversation and reflection on the *Daily Texts* for May 14, 2005, (the same date as our Annual Meeting that year) the decision was made to draw up plans for a new building to more effectively present the message of Jesus Christ.

The new building is truly a multi-purpose facility. Not only will there be a chapel on the main floor, the lower level will provide a dedicated space for ministry to our youth. The adults and seniors especially will benefit from several additions. Restrooms will be located on each level. An elevator will be accessible so that any person needing a lift can receive it easily. Windows will stretch out across the entire side toward beautiful Lake Carlos, so that anyone looking out will see the cross and the lake. Since the building will be a year around facility, we will now be able to expand our ministry with a variety of services during the winter months. The new facility represents a new chapter in the vital work of Mount Carmel.

MISSION STATEMENT

"Mount Carmel is a Christ-centered community with fellowship for all ages where the Gospel is experienced", was written by the Board of Trustees in 1987. The purpose of Mount Carmel is to create and provide Bible, Christ-centered resources that affect our daily life as Christians. The Vision statement now declares "Mount Carmel is a place set-apart where people's lives are changed through Jesus Only." Where there is no vision, the people perish we know from the Bible. But where there is no mission, the vision perishes is a recent saying that I like.

The people that we invite as teachers and preachers and staff to Mount Carmel preach Christ and Christ crucified and living. We lift up Jesus because when that happens we don't need rules and regulations. The more that we hear of Jesus, the freer we are from all the rules that we normally live under day in and day out. And that's been a very important part of our understanding of our mission.

JESUS ONLY

The name of Jesus is our hope. His name is essential. That is why we have the "Jesus Only" song. One time when Sonja was talking to us at the campfire, she said, "When I first came here I didn't like that song very well, but the longer I stay here, the more I love that song because it keeps us on focus." Jesus, that's what Mount Carmel is all about. When I preach on any Sunday morning, and wherever we go to preach or teach, Jesus is our focus and the only reason for the existence of Mount Carmel.

On the eve of Reformation Day, October 31, 2007, I was sitting in cabin #29 that was remodeled back in 1993. That was the first year in which we were debt-free of any bank loans. As I looked back, I thought Re-formed. Re-forming is what the Lord does at Mount Camel. Cabins are still being reformed. Now new ones are being built. Then came the Lodge. And now the Chapel. When the old Miller Chapel began to be demolished in October to make way for the new Learning Center and Chapel, I cried. I knew of so many blessings that had taken place in that space in the short 24 years that

Sonja and I have served here. How many more happened in all those years before?

The Lord uses our buildings, but it is the Christ-centered preaching and teaching that change us. The Holy Spirit brings Jesus to life as these words are heard and reflected on by us. Jesus is experienced in fellowship with each other as we share His Word together. What our Lord does through Mount Carmel will not change as long as we are committed to letting Jesus speak his reforming message to us and sharing our experiences of His Word in our lives.

> *'When I am lifted up,' Jesus said, 'I will draw all people unto myself.'*
>
> (John 12:32, NRSV)

We lift up Jesus. He does the reforming and it is Him that we praise.

Chapter Seven

Sonja Hinderlie

Sonja's story is full of feelings—sadness, bewilderment, confusion, hilarity, happiness and joy. Obviously, I have edited our conversation into script. Read her story and enjoy!

Sonja's Story

We moved from Wisconsin to Minneapolis, when Johan accepted the Call to work at Golden Valley Lutheran College. He was very excited to work with college kids at GVLC and to be in charge of church relations for nine months. He was also called to be the director of Mount Carmel for three months in the summer. To be considered for leadership at Mount Carmel, to spend summers on a beautiful lake in a summer camp was just kind of a plus, a "Yes!" Luther Lerseth, who had been the camp director, had gone back to his native Canada. We thought the plan sounded like a good match for us, and a kind of position we prayed about. We believed that God had called us to this kind of ministry.

When Johan and I had the first opportunity to hear about this opportunity and consider the work at Mount Carmel, my first reaction was, this is exactly what we've been trained to do—what my whole life has been guided to do. We began to pray about this possibility and seek God's will. It was a memorable day when we received the call from President Bernt Opsal to work at Golden Valley Lutheran College and direct summers at Mount Carmel. Our prayers had been answered.

In the fall of 1984 we said goodbye to our home of nine years in Cambridge, Wisconsin where Johan served as a pastor and we moved to Minneapolis. One day we took a drive up to look at Mount Carmel I said, "I've been here before." I remembered visiting the site for an Olympics Day when I went to the Norwegian Camp back in the 1960s. I played in a soccer tournament and remember walking toward the cross by the Chapel near the lake. Looking over the lake, I thought to myself, "This is a beautiful view, and what an incredibly large lake." I had never seen anything like it. That experience and remembrance of this place confirmed that God desired us to be here. I had a clear memory of the beauty and special quality of this spot and felt God's presence.

The next time we came to Mount Carmel was early in April of 1985. We looked around the property, the cabins and the buildings. All I could think of was, how would this place be open by the middle of June? The dining hall looked like there had been an evacuation, and people had left their dishes and walked out the door—a disaster. Nothing was cared for. Everything looked horrible. That was really alarming. How were we going to open this place and even have it suitable for people to come here? It just seemed daunting, and impossible In spite of all of this, we were excited about the possibilities.

OUR EXCITEMENT

The joy of this ministry was an answer to prayer for us. I had had many summers of working at Camp Augustana at Lake Geneva, Wisconsin. Johan and I met at Holden Village, were married there, and worked there. Both of us experienced a rebirth of the Holy Spirit there. We had a heart for retreat ministry, the need for spiritual growth and Bible Study. We had personally experienced the community of Christians gathering together to celebrate the gospel in food, music, and dance, using the outdoor environment. This was a calling we both shared and believed in for people.

When we got to Minneapolis in October of 1984, we decided to rent since our house in Wisconsin had not sold yet. And this way we would know where we wanted to live more permanently. Costs of living in Minneapolis were higher than those in Wisconsin so we went north to the suburbs and we rented a house in Champlin. We enrolled our kids at Riverview Elementary school where a friend of mine was a music teacher. I searched for a job in the newspaper and found a teaching job at a nursery school three mornings a week in the projects area near downtown Minneapolis. St. Stephen's Episcopal Church in Edina supported the program. Since I had a teaching degree, I applied and got the job. It was challenging because the children were quite uncontrollable. But, they were also loveable. I worked there for three years. Additionally I worked at the college helping to set up tours for the choir and orchestra.

THE SURPRISE

In April of 1985, I had set up the weekend orchestra ensemble tour and planned to travel along, playing cello and being the spokesperson for promoting Golden Valley Lutheran College. Johan and I arranged the schedule so he would watch the kids while I was gone. We went across Wisconsin and the Upper Peninsula ending up in Detroit, Michigan.

On Saturday night, Johan called me saying, "The College has closed." I said, "What! The College has closed!?" "What does this mean?" He said, "It means the College is literally stopping its operation."

The really strange thing was that next morning I was to give a temple talk about Golden Valley Lutheran College to this large church in the Detroit area... I didn't know what to do. What should I say? Johan had said, "Don't say anything about the college being closed." I said, "What do I say? How can I promote Golden Valley when it's closed?" And he said, "Well, you'll just have to pray that God will give you the right words."

Sunday morning, I spoke to the values of attending Golden Valley Lutheran College as best I could, all the time carrying this strange sense of wondering what the future held. I had to bite my tongue and hold back the reality that the school had now closed. Plus I couldn't tell any of the students who were on this tour that it was closed.

We did not even realize the implications of the closing of GVLC. How did this affect the future of Mount Carmel? Would we even have our first summer there? The feeling and thinking was just as if everything we thought

God had called us to was now a big wall—a wall and no door or window. When we came back from the tour, Johan said, "Well, we'll have to move." I said, "We will?" He said, "Yes, they won't guarantee any salaries. There is no money. We'll have to move in with my mom and dad." Thus began a most interesting and exciting journey.

STRANGE HAPPENINGS

We moved immediately, by May 1st, to Johan's parents' home. I remember buying distinctive cartoon sleeping bags for each of the boys to give them a sense of home wherever they were sleeping. We were in a point of transition. Each day we drove the kids up to the school in Champlin from near Lake of the Isles, while I finished the school year at the nursery school and Johan went to the college.

Johan and I walked around the lake each night ruminating and questioning and making plans as best we could. There was a huge mess at the college of which we were totally unaware. There were financial concerns that we knew nothing about. Teachers were all upset. Most everyone was upset and everybody was angry at President Opsal, the board, or anyone they could blame. Why did this happen? There were so many unanswered questions. Of course, nobody knew what was going to happen to Mount Carmel. The picture was very, very unclear.

Our oldest son, Nels said, "Mom, if God knew the college was going to close, and this was going to happen, why did he have us move here?" I said, "You know, that's a question I can't understand. God has some other plans that we can't see right now."

Of course, the Lord had other plans, even when we didn't have a clue as to the direction. But the whole experience of the college closing was such an odd thing. We had only been at the college since October. Now it was May. Who knew what was going to happen? So we walked and we prayed, and we talked back and forth about what we should do. Johan and I did not really know what was happening. We were out of the loop of information, even gossip. Maybe we were not listening for bad things.

84

After the college closing was announced, the College mortgaged Mount Carmel's property for $300,000 because the school had to have the money in order to hold a graduation for the class of 1985. The College must stay open long enough to allow these kids to be certified and finish their two-year degree, or complete their first year. It seemed right to do that, so Opsal and the GVLC Board mortgaged the Mount Carmel property. The College closed all operations with graduation of the class in May of 1985.

However, the Board decided that Mount Carmel should run its summer program. We made plans to move. We put our furniture and our belongings into Pastor Howard Sortland's garage, our pastor in Champlin, and moved to live in the director's cabin at Mount Carmel.

When Johan accepted the Call to serve the College and to direct Mount Carmel, I thought what Johan and I and our sons were coming into was an opportunity that was stable and predictable. But as I look back on my disillusionment, I realize the whole happening was in some strange way, a freeing experience. Now, we were able to make new decisions about Mount Carmel. Not knowing all the ins and outs of camp management and programming was probably good at that time. We didn't know really what had happened with the college and now it made no difference. We had freedom.

In May when the college closed, the Board of Directors made the decision to dispose of all the removable items—mattresses and furniture, office supplies and other odds and ends of things. We picked out several boxes of theme decorations and brought them to Mount Carmel that we used for many summers. These decorations gave us the idea to begin special theme night buffets on Thursday nights. Thus began the fun celebration of food and fellowship with special music, dancing, and frivolity. It was one of the beginning new signatures of our ministry. People who came from town enjoyed the meal and then the worship service which followed. This continues to this day.

OUR FIRST SUMMER

Those early weeks in that summer of 1985 are so memorable because they were really fun. Even though some of the staff from the college was depressed, God had opened up a new avenue and a new ministry, and we were fresh. We didn't have any feelings of bad experiences. Mount Carmel was just sort of like, "Okay, we can do whatever we want here. Let's see what God is going to do! We will just enjoy it."

I remember our youngest son, Jens, was really rambunctious. I was always afraid he might jump into the lake so I carried him around all summer long. He loved the staff girls and would sit on their laps twirling their hair. The staffs were like a big family those early years because we didn't have a lot of extra obligations. There wasn't a lot of administrative work. Everything was simple and easy. Johan and I and the three boys lived in that funny little cabin down there in the west end, the last one that is now a duplex. That was to be our summer house for 18 years. We had cousins and friends who would come and stay with us (The Boys have written about this), and we just had a flowing kind of time, very fluid and very memorable.

The schedule was intense because campers came in on Saturday afternoons and they stayed until the next Saturday morning—a full week. We had very little time to prepare for a new group between the times when the guests left from one week until the guests' arrival for the next week. The Staff and Johan and I needed more time to clean, to get ready, and to emotionally have a break. After the Lodge was built, we decided it was saner to change the plan that had been in place since 1938 and allow the property and staff to breathe for twenty-four hours. We made a new schedule of arriving on Saturday and departing on Friday noon.

Richard (Dick) Sayther helped us with some of these ideas. He was very helpful because he would challenge us and say, "What are you doing that for?" We'd say, "Well, I don't know. This is Mount Carmel!" You know, teach the Word and preach, hold forth the Word of God. Keeping this pattern was kind of important.

But, we wanted to change the pattern and the method without losing the focus. We had so many children. All these little kids, what shall we do with them? We began to consider changing some things like schedules and programs and events and how we did ministry. Some of our expectations of what we wanted to do came about with a lot of freedom because the initial expectations we had were just completely exaggerated and unreasonable or out-dated.

TWO KEY VALUES: COURTESY AND SAFETY

A key change was that we did not want to police the behavior of every-one who came here by having all kinds of rules. Johan had discovered from other camps where he had brought youth were way too legalistic with the director spending his time talking about the rules.

We had learned that if we receive the gospel message of Jesus we are no longer under the law and do not need to have so many rules. One of our teachers, Jim Otterness, had taught us about the value of courtesy from Romans 15 as a way to live together under grace. And so we shared this with all who came, that we live in a community without a lot of rules but we ask people to be courteous to each other. But this means also that there need to be quiet times like at night so people can sleep. But we did not have to impose a "lights out" plan since we left this to the freedom of the guests.

The other value is safety. This was obvious to all of us since the lake has dangers as do the hills and woods. For example, after we received the gift of a paved road we wanted to allow bike riding on the grounds. But after one child was hit by another boy on a bike and we had a few other close calls we had to eliminate bikes from the grounds for safety reasons. The kitchen is another place where the value of safety has to be held up very high.

But it has been amazing that we could run the place on these two values. But these only work because we make sure that our teaching and preaching lifts up Jesus and living under the power of His grace.

PEOPLE WHO HELPED US

Ruby and Les Larson, from Fremont, Nebraska were of enormous help that first summer. They knew things we didn't know. We didn't know anything about maintenance, anything about the cabins, how to run the dishwasher, nothing. We didn't know where the water lines were. We were left to our own ingenuity and resourcefulness. We had to learn the process as we went, and these two were very encouraging. I would go into Alexandria with Ruby and we went to garage sales, trying to find things for the cabins, because there was no budget for much of anything. In later years, Jan and Jerry Lang were the saviors of Mount Carmel in the maintenance area. They came and worked so hard for four days and with such dedication. It was awesome. Phil Jesness also volunteered and helped out and always gave us the proper perspective of everything. Phil kept us sane in the midst of these times. These were some of the important people in our ministry. The list could go on!

As the first summer ended, I think we canceled one week because there just weren't any registrations. Financially, from the talk of things it sounded like probably Mount Carmel would have to close after that summer of 1985. The Camp was there to serve. And to do that, we needed more registrations and some additional donations. But, Mount Carmel made it through the summer of 1985. And now, the school was closed. The month of September was upon us, and the camp was closed.

THE NEXT YEAR

The question now was what are we going to do? I remember we lived at Loddigs' with Herb and Edna gone for the month of September, and at Johan's parents' home in October. We knew we needed to have a permanent place to live. The boys were enrolled in the Robbinsdale school district. Our pastor, Rev. Howard Sortland at Servant of Christ Lutheran Church in Champlin, Minnesota was very supportive to us. I appreciated his kindness beyond words. We had been worshipping with his congregation, and helping him with this ministry. We ran a program for youth on Wednesday nights, Johan preached some Sundays and I directed the choir. I continued to teach at the nursery school and the kids were in school. In November of 1985 we made an offer on a home in Robbinsdale, moved in and kept on working. Even though the College was closed, the Lutheran Bible Institute was still in operation as a corporation. The Board appointed Johan to be the interim president of LBI.

A Big Summer

The summer of 1986 came. Since Johan was the LBI president, he arranged for me to be in charge of the summer ministry at Mount Carmel. We made plans for the summer program. Staff personnel were interviewed by me and hired. Johan and I worked together on the programming. Guests arrived. The summer program moved along. We invited some new people to be on the faculty that had a strong biblical teaching skill. One of these people was Marva Dawn. A prolific writer and wonderful teacher, Marva brought a fresh vision to Mount Carmel and people were encouraged in the Word through her teaching. We began a concert series on Saturday evenings that brought in more of the local folks. We continued to expand the Thursday night buffets with great food and entertainment thanks to our cooks Evie, Nancy Lund, Kathy Frank and others.

Pastor Jim Bjorge of Fargo, ND came and preached carrying the torch of proclamation. Herb Loddigs was one of the main teachers from GVLC/LBI that continued each summer at Mount Carmel until his death. Gracia Grindal, Edna Hong, and Ingrid Trobisch were some of the faculty that became mainstays at Mount Carmel throughout the years. Jim Otterness of Odessa, Texas brought his wonderful Bible Studies to Mount Carmel staff and guests. John Ylvisaker, musician, came in these early years and has continued to offer his gift of music to Mount Carmel to date. We also began the weekly Classical Music Recital. The Talent shows, water carnivals, and youth programs were also established. The style of morning Bible Studies was the same as it had always been at Mount Carmel since the beginning, with the exception that we had only one morning teacher and one evening preacher. The second half of the morning was a discussion hour; a chance to share and integrate the person's life and faith, surrounded by prayer. This was the key to the mission of "Jesus Only" in these morning studies.

Karla Rau, a friend from New York State came and worked with us as an administrative assistant in the summer of 1986. She was integrally involved in helping to pull everything together, especially with guests, donors, and in the process of "saving Mount Carmel" which began that summer. She worked for five or six consecutive summers. Her hard work and dedication was so appreciated!

One of the great successes of 1986 was that we were able to increase the number of people using Mount Carmel by about 900 guests to a total of 1600 people. This was so amazing. So many people got excited about this place and were willing to come here even when it could be cold and they had to take showers in old fashioned shower houses. At the end of the summer though we had some great news. Mount Carmel's revenue in 1986 was $47,000. And it only cost us $36,000 in expenses.

BUYING THE LAND

With possible bank foreclosures against the property, friends of Mount Carmel knew we needed to do something to secure the future. A meeting was set in early August to establish a steering committee. Out of this meeting and discussions a letter was sent out to all of the Mount Carmel mailing list.

The letter was a simple letter. It basically said, "Let's save Mount Carmel. Without immediate financial contributions, it's possible that Mount Carmel will not survive. The land and buildings may be under litigation even now because the mortgagers were saying; we need this property to pay off the debts of the College and Mount Carmel itself."

The letter proved not to be an easy task. We didn't have computers and address labels. We were using an old-fashioned typewriter and running letters off on the mimeograph machine. We basically sent out letters signing our names one at a time. We had experienced helpers like Russ Helgeson who knew about fundraising and offered their counsel and advice. We raised $150,000 through the mail.

In the fall a governing board was created from the steering committee and met once a month. I was appointed President of this Board since Johan was President of LBI during that time. Johan attended these monthly meetings and I recall spending as much time in prayer as in conversation about what the next step should be!

I began the legal work to set up a nonprofit status for Mount Carmel. I knew nothing about legal work and the process. But someone had to do it. I kept saying, "What am I doing in this lawyer's office? I am just a musician! I know nothing about this." But, no one else had the time, and we didn't have the money to buy the legal work. So I learned what was necessary and did it!

Chuck Blastervold from Cannon Falls, Minnesota was on our Board. Chuck was a banker and helped me with suggestions and paper work. I remember meeting with a lawyer in St. Paul who arranged the whole non-profit status. Now we were a bona fide organization, and we had our Board of Directors. The Board would meet together regularly, sometimes weekly, and we would watch and pray, watch and pray!

TAKING OVER THE PROPERTY AND THE DEBT

Two summers had gone by and we came to December of 1986. We had this money, $150,000, and we needed to be raising more money. Now we wondered what we should do with this money since it was not enough to pay off the whole debt but that was what people expected we were going to do.

We developed a plan of action. We told people who supported us, "If we can work a deal with the Golden Valley Bank, we will form a new corporation and transfer the property to this new ministry." The promise is, "If we can't negotiate and buy and form a new Mount Carmel, we'll send your money back." All we had for records were handwritten addresses of everybody and what they had given. It was really just a little black book with all the names in it, nothing very sophisticated but the record keeping was open and honest. Ernest and Elizabeth Bakken were so helpful in this process. Time was rolling on, and it seemed that God was teasing us. Soon it would be Christmas and we had heard no decision from the bank. On the thirtieth of December, the bank called and we arranged a meeting for the last day of the year. We signed the papers to agree to put $75, 000 down and assume a loan. This was the beginning of a new age and a promising future for Mount Carmel. It would survive! God's hand had been upon Mount Carmel all of these years, and it was going to continue to be a place for many to come and experience the living Word of the Gospel!

Mount Carmel Ministries officially inherited the indebtedness on March 17, 1987. First we had a $325,000 mortgage to the Golden Valley Bank. In addition we had a $300,000 loan against the property by the American Lutheran Church.

But to get all this done, the ALC had to make a big decision. Chuck Blaster-vold and I went down to the office of the ALC. Pastor Arnie Thompson and Johan had also been involved and Arnie paved the way to an agreeable working relationship with the ALC. We were able to negotiate an agreement attached to the loan. Chuck said to the loan officer in the ALC, "This is our situation. We have this new organization and our plan is to buy out the Mount Carmel property. Would you give us a break with our financial plan? Is there any way the ALC could forgive the $300,000? Would you consider anything like that?" The Church leaders needed to think and consult on that question.

Later, they came back and said, "We won't demand payment right now, but if you sell this property to anyone else, or if in ten years you can't make a go of Mount Carmel as a ministry, then the loan is reinstated and you must pay it off fully." The agreement was, "If you can maintain a ministry for ten years, the loan and interest will evaporate." It was the best deal you can imagine. What a gift to us from the church and what a trust! We got all of the paper work in writing— fully documented. I remember distinctly going with this farmer banker who was on our board, just a great man of prayer, both of us saying, we must make these financial arrangements and this new Mount Carmel Ministries corporation work.

Because Johan was the president of LBI, he got paid from that Corporation. The Lutheran Bible Institute was like a hand with several fingers One of the fingers was Mount Carmel, one of the fingers was *Psalm of Life*, one of the fingers was the Bible Study Correspondence courses, and another finger was preaching, teaching, reaching Seminars, and one of the fingers was the College itself. So Johan had two, Mount Carmel and the *Psalm of Life*. There was some money coming in for *Psalm of Life*. It was a popular radio program, well known and respected. The program aired on many stations but the best was WCAL, the St. Olaf College radio station, and people sent money in to the LBI for its support.

Financially Mount Carmel remained in a survival mode from 1987 to 1992. We didn't really know if we would make it year to year. Servicing the debt monthly was a challenge. We had wonderful programs and the ministry was excellent. But, at the end of each year we had some anxiety. And then, God always amazed us with His grace and made it clear that God's hand was upon Mount Carmel for good. Why was it always so hard to trust His benevolence?

The great blessing came in 1992, and that story has been told by Johan in another chapter. We were debt-free by 1993! By 1997 we had made it through ten years, and the $300,000 loan and interest from the ALC, which was now the ELCA, was forgiven and gone.

OFF SEASON OPPORTUNITIES

In January of 1987, I became the manager of the St. Anthony Park School of Dance in St. Paul. I was invited by my friend Sarah Quie to teach and help out while her husband, Joel was serving a church in Pittsburgh, PA. I loved this work, having operated a dance school previously. I enjoyed the teaching and the diversion for me was wonderful. I taught classes and managed the school for 13 winters. It was a nice complementary position during the school year to Mount Carmel's summers, so it worked out well. I purchased the school from Sarah in 1993 and owned it until 2001. Of course, all this time I continued to work with Johan at Mount Carmel serving as the Program Director which was part time work. I thank God for giving me this opportunity at the dance school.

MOUNT CARMEL LIFE STYLE

We came to open Mount Carmel on Memorial weekend each year to begin the new season. Our boys were in public school in Robbinsdale but they were here for the summer. As they grew in years of maturity and into sports, they didn't want to stay here the whole summer, so then they stayed in Robbinsdale. Those were hard years. It was uncomfortable for me to have them away from us. They stayed with my sister and her family in Brooklyn Park. I knew they were happy in their sports and we were very consumed with the people and the activities of the schedule. We had to take our vacations during the fall or winters of the year with our family. These were wonderful and memorable.

The greatest benefit for our family at Mount Carmel was the relationships with the staff who were like their older brothers and sisters. A lot of good mentoring happened between the boys and their peers. I think some of their people skills which they have today, and their enthusiasm for ministry came through the years at Mount Carmel. So I think overall the experience for our sons was positive. Whenever my parents were around for a couple of weeks the boys had someone else to watch over them and give them special attention. In later years, my parents were able to commit more time to being at Mount Carmel. This was terrific to have them there to share their gifts. Now my mother has become an integral part of this ministry for which we rejoice! She has written about the music programs that have developed over time at Mount Carmel and with her enthusiasm and efforts, these programs have grown.

SUMMER OF 1987

The summer of 1987 was the first summer as the Mount Carmel Ministries organization. We had a good summer program planned. Registrations came in slowly. We recruited staff through the Camp Fairs at Concordia, Augsburg and Moorhead State. I trained staff while Johan worked with programming, with teachers and speakers. When Johan and I attended a conference of any kind we would look and listen to a speaker, and ask them if they would consider Mount Carmel. Many new speakers and teachers came as a result.

We found people by recommendation and by hearing them ourselves, like Diogenes Allen from Princeton Seminary. We were at Chautauqua, New York, heard him speak, and I said, "We've got to get him at Mount Carmel." We asked him to come and he was with us seven years. He has been one of the most fabulous teachers we ever had here at Mount Carmel, well loved. He would still be coming if it weren't for his leukemia, and death.

THE WELCOME HOME RETREAT HOUSE

The new house came through an experience with Prof. Gracia Grindal. While she was with us as a teacher for one of the weeks, she visited at our director's house.

We had been living in that old place—that is what I called it, where we lived for many years on the west end of the campus. We'd invite the faculty down one night a week usually and we'd turn off all the lights. We were embarrassed for it frankly and honestly. I burned candles everyplace so they couldn't see how bad it was. But the house smelled of mildew and there were mice. It was in bad condition simply because it was old. When she sat down she said, "I can't believe you are living in a place like this. This is horrible. This is substandard. We need to build a new house for you."

Years previous to this conversation, maybe in 1989, one guest Johan had met on a tour to Israel said that she wanted to build a house for us. The money would be in her will—maybe $40,000 for a future house. Gracia had heard about this gift and she said, "This is ridiculous. As long as we are going to do some capital building, let's build it." She is the one who voiced the need and who raised the project up for planning and didn't let it go. The Board then got the help of a Proclaimer and builder, Joe Giroux, who volunteered to supervise the whole project so that we could save money on construction. He worked with our architect, Lloyd Jafvert, and the outcome was a new place for housing and for ministry. We named it after John Ylvisaker's song we use each Sunday, "Welcome Home."

SLOVAKIA MISSIONS

As a child, I often reflected on the Iron Curtain and what it must be like to live under that domination. My heart seemed to yearn to find out more about the people who were subject to this regime. So, when the doors opened for us to get involved with Slovakia, my latent interest was piqued.

Our ministry to the country of Slovakia has been a huge experience and having students come to Mount Carmel has just been incredible. Since 1993, we had our first Slovakian student, Juri Sabol come to work at Mount Carmel. In 1994 Lucy Graber and Mandi Scott went and served as our missionaries at a parish in Slovakia. In 2004, Erika Estenson served as our missionary teaching English at the Lutheran Elementary School in Martin. Now we are in our fifteenth year of the Slovak Mission and Paul Blom is in his second year serving as our missionary teacher. We have had at least 30 students come from Slovakia and 20-30 young adults from Latvia and Russia. Pastor Don Richman of Eastern European Missions Networks has been a partner in this venture. What a blessing this exchange has been. This is the great following of Jesus' command to "go and tell". Who else will the Lord rise up?

LEADERSHIP

In terms of leadership, Rene Moen has been our anchor. She came in 1988 to work on our summer staff, and by the end of the summer we knew about her strong gifts and willingness. In all these years we have never had a feeling of disrespect from her. She has been totally been supportive of us. When Johan and I disagree on something, she listens and then she'll say, "Okay now, let's get on with what needs to be done." She has been the mediator for us, who totally understands, and usually offers no disagreement or negativity. She is an amazing leader and very efficient. We could turn things over to her and she would get them done. She's grown a lot in her job. She used to be very quiet and shy. Now she has really blossomed and developed her leadership skills and abilities. She has become very strong with the *Daily Texts* and she is very good with organizational management.

During her years at Mount Carmel, the Holy Spirit has touched her life. When she was in college the Spirit gave her a sense of what her life should be through a calling in a Christian community. And that spark has never left her. She has a real zeal for her calling and for being involved in Mount Carmel's ministry. Rene has probably been the most right-hand person for both Johan and me.

Of course, my mother has been a great source of endless encouragement to us in this ministry. No one has more positive energy ions than Kay. Johan's mother also gave us so much support and love and understanding throughout her years. Mike Ovikian is another cheerleader for this ministry. Jean Bierly has been a spiritual guide and marriage retreat leader with us. Jane Schuneman has shared in this ministry by opening her home to our retreats in the winter, and now she is here in the summer sharing the joy of music and ministry with us. God is full of wonders, to perform! There are so many others that could be named who have given of themselves for this mission and have loved us and shared Jesus with us. We are forever grateful for each one.

EXPERIENCES

The strongest spiritual experience I had in this ministry was when we were earnestly praying about the direction to go when we started in 1986. It was so amazing that gifts of money came in, and how the Lord saved Mount Carmel. And we happened to be there! It was really amazing. One of the most memorable times was when Courtland Agre stood up in 1992 and challenged us to give a large sum of money. (Others have told the story, so I shall not repeat it here, except to say). He gave this really "speaking in tongues speech" about debt and money. That was a moment I will never forget. Only God could make such a thing occur. Another Mount Carmel miracle!

There were times throughout the years when I have doubted God's providence and care. It is evident to me that the Lord desires Mount Carmel to exist for the nurture of his people. The way Mount Carmel has been sustained, financially and how it is grown over the years makes it clear that God has His hand on this place, for good! People often comment on the feeling they have when they come here. They sense a power of holiness of God's presence, just coming on to the property. This is a place that has over one hundred people praying for it daily. This speaks for the power of this "Holy Ground".

My own personal experience with the Lord has been remarkable. There have been so many powerful inspirations with the different worship services and different speakers. I have been so convicted by the power of prayer and the work of the Holy Spirit. A couple of years ago we had a little prayer summit. We studied Hannah. I realized then that prayer is a cry for help and God answers these prayers. Many people who came to this weekend testified to the trust for God to answer our prayers. The Taize prayer time has been a lifeline of encouragement and sustenance for me at Mount Carmel. The Healing Services on Thursday night have also given me an awareness of God's great love for each person, and the depth of healing that has occurred. The *Daily Texts* have given Johan and me such a daily support in the Word and in prayer. I love how the sharing of this Word daily taps the depth of the communion of saints. I am so grateful for the ways I have been trained in this ministry of praying Scripture through this opportunity to serve at Mount Carmel.

When we first came here I used to dislike the song Jesus Only. I thought this is just the silliest song, and I don't like the words, especially "empty dross." Now Jesus Only has become very precious to me. I've changed emotionally and spiritually.

Johan and I shared a vision of working together from the beginning of our marriage. Yes, it is often challenging to work with your spouse. Many days we cannot think of anything else to discuss, except Mount Carmel or our children! I reached a breaking point on several occasions and wanted to quit. But, God's graciousness and forgiveness continued to give me strength to serve. As it says in Psalm 51:12, NRSV, "*restore unto me the joy of your salvation and uphold me with your free spirit*". This free spirit has carried me and kept me in the faith to be able to continue.

Ingrid Trobisch (Youngdale) was deeply helpful to us. She mentored our marriage, directed us into the *Daily Text*, and a brought lot of healing and strength to our relationship. Both of us grew a great deal leading marriage retreats that were shaped by Walter and Ingrid's teachings. Thanks to Ingrid, Johan and I are in a new place in our marriage relationship. Instead of competing, there is a mutual honoring of each person's gifts and living with our differences. Being able to pray together has eased and healed many wounds. We thank God for the legacy Ingrid gave us.

In closing, my prayer now is to "fight the good fight, finish the race, and keep the faith" for as long as we are called by the Lord to be here. In His timing we will move on and others will be called to take the ministry into the future. I give thanks for God's grace, and his provision of the people needed to continue a ministry that gives God the glory and lifts up Jesus Only. Until then, we will celebrate the 70th Anniversary of this mission to families and adults with gusto and pray for the illumination of God's Word to hold forth and bring the light of Jesus' resurrection to this dark world through each one of us!

Chapter Eight

HINDERLIE BROTHERS
NELS, KNUTE AND JENS

FROM NELS

My first trip to Mount Carmel with my Dad came in the spring of 1985 when I was 9 years old. A guy named Mark Kindem who was a massive person with biceps the size of softballs worked at the camp. He told us that he ate rocks and I believed him. He was a really neat guy. He was actually a student and football player from Concordia College in Moorhead, Minnesota.

Dad was in a meeting so I was with Mark. He let me take out a tractor called the Cub Cadet. It was kind of a wet spring day in April, still cold and very damp. We were pulling a trailer loaded with junk, and I managed to jack-knife the trailer due to the muddy conditions on the hill going down to the dump. That was one of my first memories. The first years at Mount Carmel were the most influential in my own life.

Most of the staff had been students at GVLC and some were multinational. There was an amazing runner named Ali Tulu from Ethiopia. There was another named, Phea Poch, who was quiet and did not speak much English, but he had amazing stories about his experiences in Laos and Cambodia. And there was Jane Chue who was an accomplished pianist from China who also had stories about the trials of growing up under a communist regime. Of course, then there were the rest of the staff who were the usual midwestern college kids.

Mount Carmel became a place of refuge over the years—a place of retreat, a second home, my extended family. That is how I came to know this place and view it. It was a place where a community was created outside of the real world, a place where people were respected and treated equally and fairly in spite of their background, race, or social status. The camp profoundly influenced a kid who never really wanted to leave his "safety bubble" of Cambridge, Wisconsin where my Dad was the pastor of the local Lutheran Church. I had a newfound appreciation for all people and a more worldly perspective than most people my age.

There was a lot of time spent driving between Minneapolis and Alexandria. We often drove strange vehicles like a mail truck that was barely road certified as well as a variety of trucks, vans and cars. One time we drove a car with a broken window, from an errant baseball, and our dad put a sign in the back saying, "follow me to Mt Carmel." We discovered every way of getting to camp. For a short time we took the Osakis route, then the West Union route, then the Nelson route via Osakis. We could never get there fast enough.

As time went along, we kids needed rides to and from the Twin Cities. Sometimes, we simply asked a camping guest for a ride and got one. Later when we could drive, people asked us to give them a ride back to the Cities. The variety of people we rode with or gave rides to was always interesting. I remember specifically riding back and forth with Jon Moen who became Rene's husband because I was playing baseball early in the summer.

When we were younger, Knute and I were on the same little league team—the Red Sox and we had a tournament in Buffalo, MN. We were driven by Matt Anderson, who worked on staff. To drive the director's kids and their cousins to a game an hour away was a pretty good job for the evening. I cannot even imagine how many times I was on that road between Alexandria and Minneapolis.

I have driven portions of that road numerous times because I went to college at Saint John's University at Collegeville, MN. Actually on a trip to Mount Carmel in the springtime while in high school, I noticed Saint John's University and how beautiful central Minnesota is at that time of year.

We stayed with Mom and Dad from about Memorial Day through Labor Day which was always kind of difficult because it meant being away from our school friends all summer. This was okay though because we had each other and our cousins, as well as the camp friends we made over the years. We all came to expect to see each other for at least one week. We needed to make these continuous new relationships with the staff and other people because our parents were always busy. Being unsupervised a lot of the time, allowed us to create our own fun. For a while, we had to go to youth chapel but then we would either torment the staff or escape to make forts by the lake or play games. One time Jens and Knute played with fire and almost blew up a gas can. We rode bikes into the lake, even ones that did not even belong to us.

Pranks were common. We would put buckets of water on top of the staff room doorways and they repaid us by throwing us in the lake. There were always a lot of hijinks—boisterous fun and tomfoolery going on especially as we got into our early teen more mischievous years.

There was a time when we stayed out all night. Maybe staying out all night happened more than once. Yes, girls were involved. But it was more to stargaze, go for a late night sauna and swim and possibly venture into Luther Crest. The adults knew that we could be out because it was a fairly safe and insulated environment. At the same time, we boys were the locals and our parents ran the place.

During the summer, we played baseball in Alexandria and eventually would attend the high school weightlifting programs and training for fall sports. As we got older, however, more time was spent in the Cities. Being away was kind of sad, because we really appreciated the summer days spent at Mount Carmel.

The summers at Mount Carmel were fun for us three boys, but it also was work. We were expected to work; I think to keep us out of trouble. Hey, we were cheap labor. We learned to mop, sweep, do dishes, roof cabins, mow grass, put in docks, and drive the boats. You name it, we did it.

One time, we had a business called, "Bros Pizza" that we ran out of the youth chapel. We were seen as competition to the canteen so the opportunity did not last long. Actually we did not get the contract we desired. When we only received $45.00 at the end of the summer, we closed our doors. People still talk about it.

Softball was the game of the day. We had numerous match-ups pitting the pride of Cannon Falls versus the camp staff. Those were always great games. Each year we as the staff acquired a new heavy hitter. First of all was Mark Kindem, then Jon Moen, and Tracy Wensloff, a lefty, who nearly put a few in the lake, then Gary Syftested. With all these strong players we were an insurmountable force, and with the three Hinderlie boys getting bigger and better each year, I don't think we ever lost. Of course, maybe that's because Jens was keeping score.

Around 1990, soccer gained in popularity. In the World Cup final that year had Germany faced Argentina, we had one representative from each country. Two of the Ovikians—Sonya and Tomas worked at camp that summer. The interesting thing is that they were born in Germany and Argentina, respectively. Over time, the sports dynamic shifted from softball to soccer and we had the "MC World Cup" with teams from Brazil, Argentina, Germany, Cameroon, and Mexico. Of course, we boys, all took part in this as well.

Each summer we also participated in choir camp that was run by our grandparents, Kay and Dick Hoffland. Knute and I were old enough to have attended at Green Lake, Wisconsin Bible Camp and Mount Carmel. That was always a fun week and it has grown tremendously. We all had musical talent as well, even though Jens started a little off key, but he was the best athlete so he made up for it.

There was a show each Friday to wrap up the week of singing. This was a week attended by lots of family and friends. We sang about Zerubbabel, Jonah, and all kinds of other subjects. Grandma Kay would remember them all for sure.

We participated in the talent show and sometimes MC'd it. We always had some skit to get back at someone or make fun of them. One unforgettable moment was when Matt Anderson impersonated my Dad. That was really funny and spot on. We also MC'd as the Star Wars reunion. I was Luke, John Watson was Han, Jakob was Chewbacca and Knute was Yoda. It was funny. We also had sketches about "OB talk," a language taught to us by Doug Swenson, now an Alexandria local. Something about a wide mouth frog! Funny stuff.

The weekly water carnival was fun and we always were pat of it. This included the tug-o-war, the greased watermelon and fun bug races. Then there was the famous "1, 2, 3, tosses," performed so well by Tracy Wenesloff and Jon Moen during the water balloon toss, a silly game, where partners throw and catch water balloons without them breaking. Sometimes we would lose this game on purpose. There was simply the fun of being in the water. The floating dock would keep us occupied for hours. We would play tag and swim under and around the floating pontoon raft with a diving platform. That was a place for performance with jumping, flipping, and diving as well as a place of solace from the rest of the camp.

At night the place of retreat and debate was the sauna. The original one burned down in the early years and was rebuilt bigger and better. Hours were spent in the sauna to keep warm and then jump in the cool waters of Lake Carlos or just to stay up late. One time we got stuck inside the sauna for a few hours. It was the three of us as well as Andrew and Kjersten Holm. It was during the day and it might have been a self-imposed exile to get out of working. I cannot remember exactly, but we got out eventually when someone came and retrieved the log from in front of the door.

We also learned to fish and water ski and tube really well. We all became prolific water skiers and would always take every opportunity we had to be on the water. Trying to stay on the tube while the driver made every attempt to buck you off was always fun. Jens was a glutton for this type of punishment and very good at these water sports, too, of course. Our cousins, Sam and Josh Graber, and Jakob, Erika, and Jon Estenson as well as John and Andy Watson were always our "partners in crime." It was never boring, and there was never a dull moment.

I suppose the nastiest thing we ever did and got away with was ringing the bell at LutherCrest. The straight forward "attack by forest path" was the best. But, we also came by road, and we came by sea. One particularly foggy night we used rowboats and canoes and swam in from their diving dock.

One time my friends from school Jack Ruegsegger, Nick Levens, and Andy Hyser and I rang the bell three times in one evening. We hid on the roof of their main building and after the initial bell ringing, avoided their "sentries" and rang it not just one more time, but twice more! For that prank we had to apologize. It kind of stopped after that. That was easily the biggest accomplishment!

We also played a game called Romans and Christians or KGB which depicted what it might be like to be a persecuted Christian. It was played at night. In REALITY, I think we persecuted the staff who was the alleged KGB spies or Roman soldiers. They were to capture the Christians, the kids led by the Hinderlies who resorted to more rebel or guerilla tactics. We won this too and eventually had to stop playing because the staff was overrun by the perceived "minority." In the end, I think that Capture the Flag was a more appropriate and fair game for everyone.

Mount Carmel shaped our lives. As I said before, the camp experience profoundly influenced me as a 9 year old kid who never really wanted to leave his "safety bubble" in Wisconsin. But as the years went by I had a newfound appreciation for all people and a more worldly perspective than most people my age. And, I have a love for Jesus!

From John Watson Friend of the Hinderlie Boys

I first traveled to Mount Carmel with Johan and Sonja and the Hinderlie boys, and my brother and sister—so there were eight of us in the car. We made the trip after a Joyful Voices Friday Night performance in Green Lake. I think Jens slept on the floor by Sonja's feet! The rest of us slept on a makeshift bed in the backseat with all of the luggage on the backseat floor. I think we drove all night. I remember waking up as we pulled up the hill to the director's cabin.

Right away we met some special people such as Ali Tulu and Phea. Everyone was very welcoming. We were treated just like more Hinderlies. Most of the staff believed we were cousins. I think we stayed for two weeks, or maybe even a month. My folks drove up from Cambridge, Wisconsin, to pick us up. What fun! I shall never forget it!

Many years later, my brother and I worked in the kitchen, because the chef named Nancy Lund got married. We drove from Door County, near Green Bay across the state and up to Alexandra. Our car had a bad radiator, so we had on turn the heat when it was 90 degrees our and we were sitting in traffic in the Cities. I thought we would have died!

Finally the Joyful Voices program was moved to Mount Carmel and we'd go up for choir camp and then stay a week, or sometimes two or even more. Usually we stayed one week because our folks would come up on the Friday for the performance and then stay the week with us. We would be like any other choir kid for the first week, but then when we stayed longer, we would be "on staff" cleaning the kitchen after dinner, doing dishes and all such work.

Our dad would hang out with Johan. We would hang out at the campfire or go to the sauna. I remember the time the sauna burnt. That was distressing. But then the camp people rebuilt it and in some degree normalcy returned. What would Mount Carmel be without the sauna?

The Watsons were at the camp as extra Hinderlie kids, and it was great. We grew up out on a farm in Wisconsin, but all of our town friends lived in a resort town on a lake, so being able to go to the lake whenever we wanted was a great thing for us. We would build forts in the woods; we once built one with some junk down on the path below the dining hall that three of us could hide in and no one could see it from the trail. I remember one year my brother got poison ivy so bad his entire face broke out and he looked like an alien or some kind of a strange being. My mother was not thrilled to hear about that.

We used to have paddle boat wars, which was great fun. All of us Watsons, and the Hinderlies—Nels, Knute, Jens, and Jake and Jon Estenson would take the two paddle boats out, often during supper, around the point below the dining hall and cabins. We'd split into teams and then ram paddle boats into each other, jumping onto the opposing boat, trying to capsize it. While looking back, that was one of the more royally stupid things I've ever been a party to, but at the time it was GREAT fun.

Sometimes, we would swim from the director's cabin to the beach, en masse, while everyone else was at supper. We'd do a lot of waterskiing, and tubing. I remember Knute had a firebug streak, including dousing sand with gas and lighting it on fire in a coffee can, then kicking it over and creating a beach of fire. Johan was furious. We got a scolding and deserved it.

We'd take lots of trips with staff to Alexandra. When we were younger, it was for trips to the DQ, or the go-carts. Once we could drive, the "gang" would drive in to DQ ourselves. A few times we took a boat to a hotel on another lake to the pizza place for Saturday Night Live and pizza.

We MC'd and participated in talent shows. One year we were the Ethiopian Choir. Ali Tulu taught us all to sing Christian songs in Ethiopian, and we would say "You have a wonderful Uncle" in Ethiopian to him, as if we were saying "Oh Captain My Captain" from Dead Poet's Society.

Early one summer, my brother and I drove up to work for a month, and we came back in August to work another month. The first month we worked in the kitchen; in fact, we ran the kitchen. That was an experience. I think I had just finished my first year of college at the University in Madison. I was definitely not used to after hours entertainment options such as sitting around the fire singing Bible songs which was a shade different nighttime activity than I was used to. But it was fun. And a great learning experience for me! Someone said in a chapel sermon "You can get to heaven and not have been to Mount Carmel, but why take the chance?" Mount Carmel changed my life in many ways and for this, I am thankful.

Chapter Nine

KAY HOFFLAND MUSIC PROGRAM

Kay Hoffland had a major impact on the life of Mount Carmel through her gift of music, and her willingness to share her enthusiasm with the campers and staff and community. Here is her story.

WE CAME TO MOUNT CARMEL

Richard (Dick) and I came to Mount Carmel through our daughter Sonja and Johan Hinderlie. When she met and married Johan, we were teaching at Millikin University in Decatur, Illinois, where Dick was professor of music from 1959 until 1991. We were never in Decatur in the summer. Instead, we did music camps all over the United States. For six weeks one summer, we did Choir Camp and Bible Studies at Camp Augustana at Lake Geneva, Wisconsin for the Illinois Synod of the Lutheran Church. All together, we were there for 10 years.

We came to Mount Carmel for part of the summer in 1985, when Sonja and Johan called us and said we were needed. They didn't have very much assurance that the camp would open. They called and asked if we would come with spiritual support and give musical leadership. They believed if they could get quality programming, then the people would still come. They were sure the campers would be forgiving of the facilities, even though the cabins were in a state of disrepair. The monies needed for maintenance in the last several years had been siphoned off to the college. There was a huge debt on the camp, and no one knew exactly how that could be managed.

There were difficult financial circumstances when Johan and Sonja came to Mount Carmel that summer. Sonja said to me one time, "We were asked to save Mount Carmel." She used that phrase: "To save it." It meant to save the land from the developers who wanted to foreclose and divide the acreage into lake home lots. The real estate agents and land developers were very eager to get the land and the Mount Carmel property.

Lake Carlos is pristine. There was no other property like it at that time. It was in demand. The land on the lake was pretty valuable and it was uniquely attractive. There were many people who had been spiritually blessed by Mount Carmel, and they wanted to save it for the purpose it was designed for back in 1938: To teach God's Word and to be a place for people to come and have spiritual nurturing. Mount Carmel on Lake Carlos from the beginning was a place set apart for the Lord's work. Prayer and trust were the ingredients that saved the Camp.

ONLY AS VOLUNTEERS

We were already teaching with Paul Christiansen. We had about seven weeks of teaching to do in the summer, so we just came here, and I think we stayed no more than two weeks. We did music instruction every night, and a little junior choir workshop over a weekend and the Sunday Service. We wanted people to know that we were having programs and evening worship with different preachers. The teachers and preachers came for very little remuneration.

Dick and I said we would always come only as volunteers, and that's what we have done all these years. We did the music program for the next six years as volunteers. We stayed a little longer if we didn't have another camp where we were doing junior choir. Sometimes we'd come back and do a week in August after we had finished with the Paul Christiansen Schools.

In 1988, we did Jonah—a really big musical with the junior choir kids for the third week only in July. We always had 9 year olds to 15 year olds for that music camp. Those were not regular campers; rather the week was special for music. When the kids came, the program was not only a Bible Camp; the week was like a junior choir singing camp. The rest of the summer and before that one week, Johan and Sonja had regular weeks of family camp which usually started the third week of June.

When the kids who are adults now come back, they are excited to talk about those years as junior choir kids. I just recently remembered a picture that was in the chapel. Those pictures are pretty interesting because they give the exact years. The chapel used to have two crosses on either side, and on that wood paneling the dates were written, 1938 on the one side, and on the other side it gave 1986, 1987, and 1988. We would always add the new number. I got the albums out this summer since some of the kids were on those pictures, and I showed it to them.

We encouraged the parents to come and their coming was exciting and rewarding. They would go to the Bible study and have a small group discussion while we had the children in the choir. The parents gathered over in the fireplace room in the former dining hall.

Before we invited the parents, we had to have counselors with the kids in the cabins. But when we had more and more parents come with their families, we felt the Lord was telling us we needed to make this a family week with a music emphasis. Sonja invited teachers also to come and do the Psalms and pictures of the parables. These were tied in to what we were doing with the children. We had that week of choir the third week of July until 2001, when we moved it to the last week of June.

FINE ARTS WEEK

We changed the format five years ago in 2001 when we started the Fine Arts Week. The last week of June was always weak in attendance. We discussed a better schedule and decided that we would move this choir week to that last week of June to generate more activity of registration. However, the new week was not quite the same program. When we started the new program, as Fine Arts Week, it would be music for everybody. There was a choir for the littlest children, a choir for the 9 through 15 year olds, a choir for the high school youth, and a choir for the adults.

Sonja and I played duets together often—Sonja with the cello and me on the piano. Sonja and I had played for a lot of weddings. We had a request from a local girl who was getting married who wished to have a trio. We needed a violinist.

We heard about a lady named Jane Schuneman who lived on a farm at Nelson, Minnesota. We went to visit with her, asking if she would be willing to join us as a trio. She said, "Yes, I'll play." She played with us at that wedding in 1988. Her violin playing fit us perfectly. After that Sonja and I would drive to her farm, and practice with her. We would play one program a year as the Mount Carmel trio. Jane's husband, Nobel, died in January 2001. The next summer we invited her to come and live at Mount Carmel because she sold the farm. Mount Carmel had just made one cabin into a duplex and she moved into one unit in 2002.

When she came to live on the campgrounds, she helped with the Fine Arts program working with us as a violinist and teacher. The program is actually very significant. The entire music program has probably been the biggest ministry for me at Mount Carmel. Because of the texts that are so powerful from the Word of God and experience in music, I have been able to share my passion for music and people.

Music and especially piano has been a way of life for me, and I am so thankful for it. I have been at that piano since I was a little girl five years old. Music has never been work; rather it has just been a natural vehicle for me. I played piano for everything. In high school, I had so many opportunities to perform and play, and also to lead a lot of groups in Luther League. Music has been my passion all of my life. When I graduated from high school in Detroit Lakes, Minnesota, I went to Concordia College, in Moorhead in order to major in music. And of course, I have loved the Lord as my personal Savior from the beginning of my life.

RELATIONSHIPS

Relationships have been significantly important for me. Even as a young girl, mother said that connecting with people was part of me. As a young person, I related easily with everybody, and the Lord just gave me that love for people. Johan and I have always had such a wonderful working relationship with the evening songs and the worship service. I always liked having things tied together, not just choosing any old hymn or any old response, but choosing music that would tie right in to what would be the theme for Johan's sermon. That doesn't happen by chance; it takes planning and study and prayer. When you have a lot of experience, you draw on that resource.

It wasn't only our music program that was fun. It was also what we did with the campers at meal time. For instance, we could just have a simple table grace or, a little hymn sing while we're at meal time. But, we did music together. When Dick wasn't able to lead any more, then Rikka, or Sonja or Johan often did the singing with me. We still carried on that same pattern at the dining hall. It's a part of us to share and draw out that fun part of people. This connects them to each other during the meal at the table. Singing at meal time is a thread that connects relationships and personalities.

I have been watching and observing these campers in terms of relationships now for many years. I have seen major changes as they have come and gone year after year, of course. You see them grow, and they come back again and again.

It's not only the guests and campers—the second thing I want to share is the staff's presence and participation in worship each Sunday. Regardless of their nationality or religious background, they are always expected to attend the service and hear Johan preach as well as sing and participate. Of course, it is understood that they can't attend all the sessions. They are encouraged to make the evening service, but it is also understood that there are ongoing chores at camp and they need a break from their duties.

Each member is also expected to sing in the choir as part of their job responsibilities. They don't have a choice, "Do I want to sing or don't I?" No question! They all participate. The reason we require them to be with in the choir is that singing builds a lot of community. I have worked with kids who couldn't even carry a tune when they came. Since we had so much experience teaching junior high and high school students, Dick and I would always work with these kids. We would work with them to come into some confidence in singing. Here at Mount Carmel they sing every Sunday and there is a purpose for their worship experience. They need the responsibility of presenting music as a member of the staff. To be welcoming people, that's one thing. But, sharing some music like this is quite another thing.

The ritual of Sunday worship, however, has great significance. Here is one example. Last summer there was a boy named Brian who was back for the third year and he had no voice. This summer, guess what happened? He had found his voice with a big smile. He now was a leader with the male section in a different way since he could sing on the melody line. He was so excited at one rehearsal he said, "Oh, we sound so good I think we should go on tour."

CONCERT SERIES

The concert series has been a major way to develop an interest in Mount Carmel. Dick and I found much reward and fun in arranging this event since 1989. The series was a special concert every Saturday night for at least six weeks starting with the first week of camp and running through August. We would fill Miller Chapel with people from the area as well as our camping guests.

We located groups through the year that were traveling throughout Minnesota and the USA, and we would invite them to stop here. Maybe the concert was a youth encounter group, or a choral group, or an instrumental group, or maybe just a talented couple singing and playing. The program was always something different.

I brought in a story every week to be publicized in The Echo, our newspaper in Alexandria. We had a lot of people who came from the area who had never been to Mount Carmel. We had a series of different kinds of programs, such as the Osakis Male Chorus, and the Czech dancers from St. Paul.

The groups that generated more interest and enthusiasm were always the ones from Norway, because they would perform in their native costume. They would either be dancers, or singers, or an accordion group. We had big receptions for them so that socializing could happen and it did. Where these musicians lived in Norway was also of special interest to many visitors. People talked with them about cities and locations and possible family ties. Visitors would find the musicians were from the same province in Norway where some of the relatives lived. It was a very wonderful blessing to communicate with these groups and hear their performances.

We extended a great deal of hospitality to these groups. We gave them the evening meal, and overnight lodging and breakfast. At the end of the concert, I would always announce a welcome to everyone to worship. That first summer of 1986, we welcomed Ken Medema, a visually impaired pianist. We had to show people that the camp was going to have exciting ministries which would reach out with quality programs and ministry.

One of the great pianists who visited with his father was a nineteen year old Swedish boy named Anders. He had been giving concerts across the USA. We had so many people at his concert that we didn't have enough seating room. They stayed Saturday night, but were so tired of travel; they asked if they might stay longer. They stayed another day, and we ministered to them with the *Daily Texts*. They were so interested in our ministry and fascinated by the *Daily Texts*. I explained the *Daily Texts* to them, what it was and how it was to be used. They had never heard of anything like this devotional book. The young man wanted to know more about Jesus. I sat with him in the lodge by the fireplace, and I went through the *Daily Texts* front and back. I said, "Now you just take this book as you very own." The Scripture that day was a wonderful text from John about how God loves you, and His love is for us. And so it was, we had these new guests staying on through Sunday night. They heard a great preaching, and they were absolutely moved by the Spirit of God—the Mount Carmel experience just inspired them.

The next morning when they left, he took extra copies of the *Daily Texts* for his girlfriend in Norway, and one each for himself and his father. When they got home, his dad called us. I remember we were having an evening dinner and Johan called me to the phone, with his dad on the phone saying that he wanted to tell me that on the trip to Norway, Anders had read the *Daily Texts* all the way home.

We have these great opportunities to lead people to faith, and let the Holy Spirit work, and learn about Jesus. Jesus Only is our underlying theme. The perfect study of the Good News of Jesus and His love is what this retreat center is all about, and that is why we stay right in the Word. As long as we can hold onto that strong emphasis of keeping God's Word, and people keep coming and wanting to hear God's Word, the Holy Spirit will work. That's been the history of Mount Carmel for seventy years. In spite of the hard times, the leadership and the staff and the messengers have never deviated from the message of the Gospel.

One of the best of the Concert Series has been the Barbary Coast Dixieland Band from Minneapolis. How they happened to come to us is an interesting story. Johan and Sonja presented a program on Martin Luther and his wife, Katharina von Bora (Kathie) at a church where the Dixieland Band played as part of the program. They invited the Band to come to Mount Carmel, and they have been coming for several years in August. They play on Saturday night and present the worship service on Sunday.

BEST EXPERIENCES

In 1998, John and Jim Bjorge spear-headed the fund drive for the sleeping wing to the Lodge. Many people were present on the Saturday night when Dick and I were honored with "Room Number One" given by all of these families and friends, and lots of Millikin University people. Many people had given donations to reach the $30,000 for that room. That was a very strong and powerful night for me. Each one of those rooms was given as an honor and memorial for someone. Paintings were made for each room, and a label outside each door recognizes the donor for each room.

In 1999, when Sonja, Rikka, and Elsa, my three daughters, and I did the program; that was a powerful night. All the grandkids were present, Dick was in a wheelchair, and the program was beautiful. That was a beautiful experience because of the family involvement. It has just been very deep and meaningful, because we shared Jesus and spiritual growth through music.

I have been able to feel the heartbeat of the camp as I buzz around the dining hall or move over to the chapel to the piano to lead us in singing. Knowing the workings of the camp inside and out has meant a wonderful focus for me. I am so thankful for this enthusiastic feeling because I had the same experience in Millikin University and the church we belonged to in Decatur, where I felt the heartbeat of the city. The focus gives you direction for your daily journey, and really, I just keep focused on the Lord working through me.

JOHAN AND SONJA AS A TEAM

When Sonja graduated from high school in 1972, she answered an advertisement in The Lutheran Standard for a job at Holden Village in Chelan, Washington. Rev. Carroll and Mary Hinderlie had gone to Holden in 1963 as camp directors and developed the Lifestyle Enrichment Programs.That summer, Johan, a senior at Luther Seminary in St. Paul, was visiting his parents at Holden. Sonja met Johan, fell in love and they were married the next year in 1973.

After several years of working in parish ministry, Johan and Sonja were excited to have the opportunity to serve Mount Carmel because of its mission and purpose even though the camp didn't have a lot of beautiful buildings. It would have good programming and solid preaching and teaching of God's Word.

Dick and I were excited to be a part of their ministry. What they asked us to present was exactly what we had been doing so it was a natural fit for us to join into the camp's programs. After all the years in music and camping schools, I continue to feel that the intentionality of inviting people and encouraging people and nurturing people at Mount Carmel in the Word of God is so vital.

For example, the Lord has a special place for pastors to come to Mount Carmel for renewal and refreshment. Pastors and their spouses need a place to take time to be well fed physically and spiritually. God wants missionaries to come and rest, and be renewed to go out from this place to the world. My vision is for people to have that camp experience so they are equipped with the knowledge of the Word of God. God's people experience equipping and commitment through community and music and through the environment.

Mount Carmel is unusual in many ways. Take for instance, the beautiful pristine Lake Carlos—the lake to me is a huge blessing, with the reflections, the white capped waves, the sounds, the stillness, the morning fog and the mist. The grounds have a personality. The camp has a restful environment. That is why the buildings must look renewed and refreshed. I always say the thing about vision and purpose is that everything is in God's timing and has been with His blessing. I often thank the Lord for my great memory of music, and the joy of being able to share that gift of music with all the wonderful guests who are Mount Carmel people.

Chapter Ten

Administrative Director Rene Moen

As we began Rene's story, I said, "Rene, as I watch you buzz around the office, I sense you feel the heartbeat of the camp. You know the workings inside and outside. What has that meant for you?"

Rene responded, "It fits my personality to be the connector of people and programs, to be the person who can answer any and all questions. I always feel renewed at the end of a summer. I don't have the chance to attend all the Bible studies. I go to some of the worship services. The things we do as a staff—the Bible studies, and prayer times are very uplifting. And, of course, our social times are great, too."

She continued, "I truly do love people, and I am an extrovert. I get my energy from being around other people. I do meet people well and I always have a smile and an uplifting word for them. When the campers return, 'Welcome back,' I say, and 'Oh, it's just good to see you!' I really am delighted to welcome people."

Searching for a Job

I came to Mount Carmel in June of 1988, when I was a senior at Mankato State University. A friend of mine asked me what I was going to do for a summer job. I didn't know. Each summer for the last six years, I worked as a bank teller in the small town of Glenville in southern Minnesota where I grew up.

I said I was interested in doing something different. My friend, said, "Well, how about working at a camp for the summer?" My first reaction was, "No, way!" I thought it would be a kid's camp, and I said, "No, I don't want to stay in the same cabin with homesick kids, and have them crying to go home!" She said, "No, no. It's a family camp so you don't stay with the kids. You have your own place to stay and all of that." And I said, "Okay, I'll think about it."

I called Sonja who was Program Director. She had all her positions filled for the youth staff, except the week before she had gotten a phone call that someone couldn't come. She interviewed me over the phone and offered me the job. I had never been to Mount Carmel until the day I drove there to begin my work.

I didn't know what my job would be exactly, but I knew I would be working with the elementary kids. And that's what I did the whole first summer, as a youth staff member. In the fall, I went to Roseville, Minnesota and got a job in a clothing store. But, I really did not like the clothing business, and so I just worked there until the end of May. I was in contact with Sonja, and I asked her if I could come back. She said, "Yes." They knew I had some skills in administration, so I worked in the office the next summer. But, it really was just a summer job.

I began helping Sonja with registration of campers. In addition I took care of the financial part of registration. I collected the money from the campers for their registration. I also counted the worship offering, and took the money and checks to the bank for deposit. Back then, Mount Carmel didn't have bookkeeping in house. The bookkeeper was from the GVLC. I sent all of the financial information to her.

In the fall of 1989 and the winter of 1990, I went back to Mankato State. I did graduate work in Special Education, because I have a degree in teaching. I didn't study business, because I didn't know I would continue working at Mount Carmel. I was still planning on a teaching career. However, MSU didn't offer any graduate classes in the summer, so I went back to work for Mount Carmel again as an office worker. The job was for the summer. But then in the fall of 1990, Sonja and Johan asked me to work for them full time in a yearround position.

THE LORD CALLED ME

At this time, Mount Carmel was its own corporation. It had separated from GVLC. But, there was no office at Mount Carmel in Alexandria. Instead, we had an office in Robbinsdale, Minnesota. I was the secretary/receptionist, but I really did just a little of everything.

Jon Moen and I met the first summer I was at the camp in 1988. He was on the summer staff, and that was his third summer. Jon was studying at St. Olaf College to be a teacher. After graduation and before we married, Jon began a job at the Delano Middle School as the computer technology coordinator.

We were married in December of 1991. After our girls, Kjersten and Anika, were born, I moved to 80 % from fulltime. I have been at Mount Carmel now for over 19 years. It's a funny thing. When I came that first summer for a twelve-week commitment, I never imagined that I would still be here in 2006, 19 years later.

I believe now, the Lord called me here. Mount Carmel is the place that changes people's lives, and it really has touched mine. There is something special about it. It's holy ground. It's just been fun to be part of a place that has grown, had struggles, but lots of joy as well.

I look at my work at Mount Carmel as a calling. I think it's true of lots of people. Something starts as a job, and eventually they find it was the Lord's calling to them. That's the way it has been for me. As I look back on these years what has given me the most reward is to be part of the leadership staff. It is the staff that continues to maintain this place set apart and focus on the spiritual tone that is "Jesus Only." Mount Carmel is a place that doesn't get caught up in political or social issues. We call Mount Carmel a renewal center. I believe that's what it does for people. Many people have told me how their life has changed and whole families have changed because they spent quality time at Mount Carmel.

119

LEADERSHIP ROLE

I have under my years of leadership several major accomplishments that I think are crucial. I help with the brochures and the newsletters. Keeping people informed about Mount Carmel is a big job. I stay in touch with the whole marketing area. Where people are living and what form of medium they are receiving, whether emails or phone calls or written materials are vital.

The whole area of advertising is a challenge because people have so many choices on how they will spend their limited amount of vacation time. What attracts them to us? We have tried many different approaches. We have tried advertising through churches and different groups. But really what is the best way of getting people to Mount Carmel is through current guests telling their friends or bringing their friends. The word of mouth has proven time and again to be most successful way of marketing.

Mount Carmel is a place that is hard to describe on paper. People who come here feel a calling to study and participate. A lady who has come to Mount Carmel for years once told me she believes people are called to come to Mount Carmel. God works on people's hearts and in their lives. The Lord calls them to come here for their week of vacation and renewal.

The *Daily Texts* ministry has brought people to Mount Carmel. We have been doing our own edition of the *Daily Texts* for 10 years. The *Daily Texts* itself has probably brought maybe two or three families. It crosses over minimally. Obviously, not everybody who reads the *Daily Text* comes to Mount Carmel, but not everybody who comes to Mount Carmel reads the *Daily Texts*.

How many copies were printed for this year of 2006? That's a very timely question, because 32,000 copies arrived at Mount Carmel yesterday. This year for the first time we received a request from a chaplain in the military in Iraq for 7,000 books. Otherwise, we would have printed 25, 000 copies. I am the project manager for the *Daily Texts*. I coordinate all the assembly process of the book. I do a little bit of marketing, but my job really is to put the book together, to work with the book designer and the printer. I am working now with the military chaplain based in Bloomington, Minnesota, and how best to transport these 7,000 books to Iraq.

ADMINISTRATIVE DUTIES, FINANCIAL

The Proclaimers have had a significant place and position with Mount Carmel in terms of money and membership. The Proclaimer idea was the brain-child Richard Sayther. Mount Carmel has worked with him for all the years that Johan and Sonja Hinderlie have been here.

Proclaimers donate $200 or more in a calendar year to our Annual Fund. In the year 2006, we had 557 Proclaimers either individuals or households. Mount Carmel's by-laws declare that they are the owners of the ministry and that entitles them to elect the board of trustees.

Another financial task I manage along with the Proclaimers is the matching program by Thrivent Financial for Lutherans called Giving Plus. For each dollar donated by a Thrivent member, the Giving Plus program matches with 50 cents. This program began in 1999 by Lutheran Brotherhood.

My administrative duties have totally changed over the years. What I did in the early years as the receptionist and the secretary is now the task of Anji Mousseau. She has been here since 1998, and she is now replaced by Shiloy Baldwin. I still do the registration work, so that part hasn't changed. My title for work now is Administrative Director.

ADMINISTRATIVE DUTIES, RELATIONSHIPS

Relationships at Mount Carmel have always been important. Jon and I met here. That of course has been the one big blessing for me. When I think of the staff and guests and volunteers, three different areas come to mind.

The first is that around 75 percent of our guests every week during the summer are returning guests. The same holds true for the Elderversity. Very quickly you develop a relationship with the people who come year after year. It's a relationship that's based around Jesus. Everybody talks freely and openly, and it's just a great thing for me to see all these same people every year.

The second area would be all the wonderful staff people that I've met. Yes, there is a continuous turnover of summer staff every year, but we do have some returning every session. And of course, the permanent staff and volunteers are always a delight to work with.

And the third, working with the leadership of Johan and Sonja Hinderlie. This has been very meaningful for me. They are very Christ-centered. They are also very creative and spontaneous people. I think our combination of personalities works well together. Johan is more of a dreamer, which every organization needs. But I am more of a realist, which every organization also needs. We can speak honestly to each other and respect each other's opinion. I think if a person has a good working relationship with people, then you are blessed. It's just been a real joy for me to be at Mount Carmel.

Working with people at Mount Carmel has given me many opportunities to meet new people. Like I said, in any given year, about 75% of our summer guests are returnees. That means we are getting one out of four new people each year. We work a lot harder obviously to get that 25 % than for the 75%. We put more of our marketing budget into the 25% in order to know who they are and where they came from. We want to know how to help people to understand what Mount Carmel is, and how they can benefit from a Mount Carmel experience.

Seventy five percent of the Mount Carmel regulars are heavily committed to this place. And not only committed to come for a week, but these people year contribute financially each year and pray for the ministry, which is invaluable. Mount Carmel has been built and sustained on prayer by people who love the Lord.

Administrative Duties, Stressful

Mount Carmel can be a stressful place to work at times during the summer. I work six days a week and the days are long working intensely with people. When you live in the same community with the staff day in and day out, you really need the Lord to help you extend his grace.

Jon has given me his full support and blessing not only to work but as a calling so that my job has become a ministry for me. I am very intentional about the one day off a week that I have. We don't go up to the Lodge on that day, because if I'm around the Lodge or near the front desk people assume I am working, which is a natural assumption. So I just can't go up there on my day off.

Sometimes, I just have to be intentional about leaving camp or going into town on my day off. I don't go to our winter home in Delano, because it's a two-hour drive. We have breakfast in our cabin and just kind of relax and rest. The girls still like to go to the youth program in the morning. We drive into town and have lunch. We might just go to a park and play games or wander around town. We have a boat, and we might go water skiing or tubing. We also enjoy playing golf.

Our girls—Kjersten and Anika have been at Mount Carmel since they were babies. It really is their second home. They don't know what it's like not to go to Mount Carmel. I sense especially in Kjersten, that she is freer here to be who God made her to be. I don't know if I can even verbalize it better than that. It's just a special place.

THE FUTURE

As I have observed the campers from year by year, their needs and desires have changed. The camper today is looking and asking for something different than they did in the years when I first came. They are looking for better quality housing. They want a little more refined camping experience than the primitive style which we have had in our older cabins. The primitive old cabin obviously doesn't bother the people who have been coming for 20 or more years because that's the Mount Carmel they know and love.

But, better quality housing is needed to attract the people who haven't been to Mount Carmel. The programmatic expectation of the guests has not changed. They still expect a quality of Bible teacher, a quality youth program and quality food.

I believe in what Jesus does with staff and campers at Mount Carmel. I see how the Mount Carmel experience makes a difference in people's lives. My commitment and dedication have been to the mission of renewing lives through Jesus Only.

Chapter Eleven

Irene Myhro Original Board Member

Irene (Larson) Myhro had been one of the original board members, and she along with her husband, Norman Myhro, began the International Weekend Program.

She wrote in the summer of 1961, Norman and I, with our four children, arrived at Mount Carmel for the first time. Because we could not afford a cabin, we set up our tent. We already were experienced campers. The children were ages nine, eight, five and two. Norman left early Monday morning to be back at work while I stayed at the Mount Carmel with our family during the week. Norman returned Thursday evening for a long 4th of July weekend. Pastor Herbert Malm was the business manager. His wife Evelyn Malm along with Clara Helland and Alice Strand were the cooks.

The Christian community of unconditional love that we experienced at Mount Carmel was so great that we have come every year since 1961. We felt embraced in the arms of God's love through the Word, the prayers, the Christian community and the beauty of God's surrounding creation. There was an abiding presence of God through the power of prayers of people from the past, present and yet to come. We were blessed to be a blessing. We returned home trusting God to be with us in all the experiences of our lives. God is so good. We all knew we would be back next summer. Now, we look forward to many renewal times together with friends at Mount Carmel and our four families.

There were great teachers to inspire us as the years went by. I remember Pastors Anchor Berg, A. W. Knox, Wilson Fagerberg, Herbert (Hub) Malm, Roy Bloomquist and Herbert Loddigs; Doctors C.O. Grundland and R.E.

Nelson; Ms. Sadie Ponswith and Ms. Karla Holterman. John Seagard was the Director of Music. Our lifeguards were John Malm and Michael Ovikian.

In our camping and tenting years, we were sad to see Mount Carmel not being fully used. Those years, due to lack of promotion and upkeep, the camp ended the summer season in the "red." The staff would discuss with the few in attendance the possibility of selling the Mount Carmel. It was my conviction that we could not sell what God had intended for Kingdom Work. The next summer the same inquiry continued. However, at that time Pastor Roy Bloomquist became the Executive Director of Mount Carmel. With the Lord's help and Roy's hard work and frugality, he was able to save the camp.

Our son John grew up and worked on the staff with Pastor Bloomquist for several years during the summer. John was "jack-of-all-trades" as there were very few staff people. One night he came by our tent in ghostly attire. His mission: destruction of the hornet nests.

Many people who came to Mount Carmel enjoyed fishing. Every year Norman and I bought a fishing license so we could fish the last Saturday morning. We rolled out of our sleeping bags at 5:30 a.m. We dressed quickly and quietly, and made our way to the big yellow motorboat. We moved out beyond the diving dock to where there was a "drop-off." There we caught sunfish, crappies and small mouth bass. It was beautiful and quiet as the day awakened. By 7:30 a.m., we had caught a large mess of fish, just enough for our 10 o'clock brunch. I hurried to the fish house and quickly cleaned them. Soon the camp site was fragrant with frying fish and pancakes. When we first went to Mount Carmel we were six. Then there were marriages, and grand children plus our Chinese foster son, Albert Ting. Finally, there were twenty-two of us. Others joined us on weekends.

Norman enjoyed taking the young people in camp water skiing. That was a popular sport in the late 1960's and 1970's. Of course, singing was always a part of camp life at Mount Carmel. As our growing teenagers found it difficult to be in bed at 10 p.m., we did break the rules and took our family down to the Youth Chapel basement. We sang quietly, popped corn in the fireplace and visited. One time, when Pastor Berg came around to check out the camp, he found us having a party. He joined us. Later, as times and rules changed, our parties took place in a large screened-in tent out under the stars, old and young together. We sang, ate homemade goodies and told stories.

LAND SECURED AND THE KINGDOM THRIVING

In June of 1986, Johan Hinderlie and I had lunch together to discuss the issues faced by the camp in regard to the debt owed. We both had a great, almost desperate concern for Mount Carmel. Obviously, a board had to be elected from the Mount Carmel constituency.

From the beginning, Mount Carmel had been directed by the president of the Lutheran Bible Institute, with summer camp directors and business managers appointed by the president. When the College closed, there was no one responsible for the management of Mount Carmel, and no one person to give positive direction.

God calls His people to be on boards to further His kingdom work on earth. In early August 1986 a meeting was held at Mount Carmel to elect from the constituency, a steering committee of nine people. It was with great but trembling joy that I accepted this elected position. My concern was for the on-going ministry of Mount Carmel for all people of all ages.

Later a corporation was developed. As a result, the steering committee was called the Board of Directors of the Mount Carmel Ministries. It became my privilege to serve on this nine member board for several terms. This board experience was a great faith venture, unfolding beyond the limits of the imagination.

When thinking and praying for the next board meeting or retreat, I remember the great expectation that filled my very being. Sharing fellowship with other Christians under the leadership of Johan and Sonja in Kingdom work was almost a hilarious joy. I had to ask for patience to see what God would do. Psalm 37: 7, reads, *"Rest in the Lord. Wait patiently for Him."*

Board retreats were needed to develop mission statements and new directions in ministry. New board members meant rearrangements of responsibilities. There were many presentations centering on possible master plans for the campus. Architectural plans needed to be evaluated and finally accepted. Retreats took place in Minneapolis, St. Cloud, Mount Carmel and other places as well.

Our first task as a newly elected board was somehow to acquire the money needed to hold on to the property and to operate. Through calling, $130,000 was raised, not enough to deal with both the American Lutheran Church and the Golden Valley Bank. At the October board meeting, it was suggested that we send the money back to the donors, because the financial condition looked hopeless. A committee from the Board had gone to the ALC twice. The ALC would not let the committee's big toe in the back door. Mount Carmel was an independent Lutheran movement, which had its roots in the Augustana Synod, and was in no way related to the American Lutheran Church. Because of that, it seemed there was no mercy.

The Mount Carmel board did not send the $130,000 back to the donors. It was "trust" money. On November 5, 1986, a large delegation, including Rev. Arnold T. Thompson, went again to reason with the ALC. We waited, watched and prayed. On Christmas Eve day, a call came to the home of Johan and Sonja Hinderlie. The message was simple but sweet. "The total of $300,000 will be totally forgiven, interest free, if within 10 years you are still carrying on the ministry."

Miracles began to happen. Large donations were made and matched. Large and small gifts came week after week throughout the summer of 1987. Golden Valley Bank was also kind to us. Two years were given before payments were to commence. We were able to keep the camp going and growing, manage insurance of guests and property, and began long overdue maintenance. Within ten years Mount Carmel not only paid the debt to the bank, but also raised money for the new Lodge, with beautiful dining room facilities.

International Outreach

After the election of board members on August 9th, 1986, it was obvious that nothing was going to happen at Mount Carmel for the rest of that month and maybe the season. I went to Johan and asked him, if I could bring about a group of 120 international students and families for a Bible Conference on Labor Day weekend at Mount Carmel. Pastor Johan looked at me and said, "If you want to take the risk." Of course, that response meant to me an unquestionable, "Yes!"

Over 120 international people, including students from many different countries attended. Everything was well organized and went well. The International Outreach was the first of 17 international conferences that Norman and I worked with. Four of those conferences took place on Labor Day weekends, and the other 13 were held on Memorial Day weekends.

When the new Lodge was being built, the Memorial Day weekend became a work weekend. I was privileged to cook for the helpers. We were happily blessed that weekend. Our International Students, Inc. (ISI), friends from the Czech Republic announced during the evening service that now they were believers and Christians.

Norman and I patterned the International Weekend Conferences after Mount Carmel weeks. They were really like a usual Mount Carmel week held on a weekend. The first conference we did alone, because there was no staff at Mount Carmel to help. It could have been overwhelming, but the Lord led every step of the way as volunteers stepped forward to help.

We shared wonderful meals together, had a great international talent show, and a campfire by the beach. Michael Ovikian came to Mount Carmel as a life guard in 1958 and was one of the first campfire speakers. He is still a marvelous storyteller. He has been present at every international weekend since 1986. A person came to me after a campfire service and said, "This is Martin Luther King's dream." It was an amazing grace experience. That first International Student Conference was a huge success. All were well fed spiritually and physically.

Multi Ministry Programs

Mount Carmel Ministries is involved in many different opportunities for ministry. The *Daily Texts*, a Mount Carmel version of the Moravian devotional prayer book, is published by the thousands. It is used in homes, churches and in the armed forces. Entire Evangelical Lutheran Church of America Synods are using the *Daily Texts*.

Elderversity is a fall program, usually during the months of August, September and October, especially designed for the older folks. During the summer, beginning in June, there are pastoral and theological retreats, marriage retreats, prayer retreats, pre-marital retreats, and family retreats. A new outreach ministry has developed in Slovakia that is exciting.

When summer and fall programs are finished, the Hinderlies are out "On the Road", serving the Lord somewhere. It could be a retreat in Arizona, a trip to Europe with a group, or a teaching assignment in a special place. There are weddings to officiate, funerals, promotional work, and drama productions of Martin and Katie, meaning Martin Luther and his beloved wife, Katherine. I am so proud of them and thankful for them.

Our prayer for Mount Carmel is this: May the loving Holy Spirit touch the hearts of people outside of the Kingdom, so they can believe in our loving Savior Jesus Christ, and come to rest in the love of our Heavenly Father. We are thankful for all the called servants of God who keep the "Kingdom Coming" at Mount Carmel. We are thankful for Godly leadership and Christian Community.

As I have reflected on the work of the Board of Directors and our years spent at Mount Carmel, my greatest blessing is a growing relationship with God, the Father and His unconditional love for me through Christ. I look about me and see this love in others. What beauty it is to behold the reflection of God's love in His people. We believe Mount Carmel truly is "a little bit of heaven on earth now and is a foretaste of the Heaven that is to come."

Chapter Twelve

JOHN AND JAMES BJORGE

FROM JOHN BJORGE

We came to Mount Carmel in the 1930's and early 40's with our parents—Johs and Esther Bjorge. The camp was on beautiful Lake Carlos, and it was a terribly dusty road to get there. I remember we drove from our home in Windom, Minnesota. Our Dad's sister, Auslag, was married to Art Hasle who was the Business Manager for the LBI of which Mount Carmel was a part. That was our direct connection to the camp.

Our Mom and Dad were very devout Christians. They set a good example for their three sons—James, Mark and me not only by what they said, but also by what they did. Later on both Jim and Mark became lifeguards at Camp.

In those early days, there were rather strict rules—no swimming on Sunday afternoons, very modest bathing suits, and the lights were out at a certain time every night. The meals were served family style by singing waitresses. In addition, there was a canteen in the dining hall, along with a bookstore in the lounge area.

Of course, we liked the swimming and the canteen. I still remember the first crush I had on a girl, and I did not have the courage to even say "hello" to her. She was Pastor Samuel Miller's daughter, Faith.

Mount Carmel has been close to my heart for many years. In 1996, my brother Jim and I encouraged the building of a sleeping wing along with the new Lodge, which had replaced the old Dining Center. I went up almost every week that summer encouraging support for the Sleeping Wing and contributing some of our money toward it. One room is in memory of our parents and our brother Mark.

The aim of Mount Carmel has always been to know Jesus and to grow in Him, becoming like Him as much as possible from head to foot. The mission is to foster spiritual growth in Jesus Christ by applying the Bible to daily life. The vision is to transform lives through "Jesus Only."

Campers in our day want more modern conveniences. Back in the early days, there were bath houses with both toilets and showers. Now each cabin has indoor plumbing, and the sleeping wing and some of the remodeled cabins have air conditioning. Think of that!

When Golden Valley Lutheran College went belly-up, we almost lost Mount Carmel because a loan had been taken out against the Mount Carmel property. A few individuals fortunately raised enough money along with a sizeable loan from the American Lutheran Church, which the Church forgave, to enable Mount Carmel to retain the property.

Mount Carmel has meant a lot to the Bjorge family—to our parents and James, John and Mark. My brother Jim has been preaching there in the Miller Chapel for many years. I have conducted and taught Bible Studies several times. Our son John who is an ELCA pastor has preached there the last two summers, and is now the vice-chair of the Mount Carmel Board of Directors. I understand he is scheduled to preach again next summer which makes me and his mother—Margaret, proud, honored and happy.

Mount Carmel's core values such as Biblically sound and evangelical have not changed thru the years, while unfortunately The Evangelical Lutheran Church (ELCA) seems to have become more liberal. Mount Carmel is indeed holy ground for me and many others, and one senses it when there on the grounds. Reverend Samuel Miller, the founder of Mount Carmel was a very handsome man with strong convictions. His song, "Jesus Only" became the theme song for Mount Carmel. It is a song I love. My hope and dream, and my prayer is: May Mount Carmel continue to be Christ-centered and Biblically sound as the leadership continues to expand its ministry.

FROM JIM BJORGE

Before 1938 when Mount Carmel Camp was launched, our family had attended the Lutheran Bible Institute's rented camp at Lake Independence west of Minneapolis, and also the camp at Lake Geneva in Wisconsin. Thus in 1938 with the birth of Mount Carmel a relationship began with us that remains strong to this day.

Early in my brother John's and my life, Lake Carlos beckoned us to enter the water to develop our swimming skills. Dad, who came over to this country from Norway at age sixteen, was a great swimmer and gymnast. I fondly recall his teaching us boys the joy of water. I guess during those early years, I remember that part of the camp more than the teaching and preaching.

However, the Bible teaching at Mount Carmel left a great impact on our parents and later, on us boys. Samuel Miller, A.W. Knock, Odd Gornitzka, Eugene Stime, Randolph, and others played a role in our faith information. In fact, Randolph left such a mark on our parents that our younger brother Mark, eleven years my junior, was given Randolph as his middle name.

As brother John and I entered our Junior High School years, we attended Mount Carmel during the youth weeks, which was the standard practice in the early days of the camp. The summer of 1955, I finished my second year at Luther Seminary in St. Paul, Minnesota. I became the lifeguard at Mount Carmel and then, I did my internship at First Lutheran Church in Alexandria, Minnesota. The next summer of 1956, I was also a member of the camp staff.

The year 1957 was a highlight summer for me at Mount Carmel. On July 3rd of that year, I had my first date with a beautiful brunette named Frances Erickson. I knew immediately that Fran was the person with whom I wanted to spend my life. However, she was getting ready to leave for California to accept a teaching job, so we had the opportunity for only a few times together before she left. It was a three day "date" at Mount Carmel that we both began to realize the Lord's hand was in this relationship. The next summer when she returned from teaching we were married and the Lord filled our lives with blessings. One year later, we came to Mount Carmel again with our first born son, Barak, and spent a week in the honeymoon cabin.

Since the day Pastor Luther Lerseth became camp director, I have had the privilege of preaching regularly at the camp and it has been a great experience. In 1997 when I retired from First Lutheran Church in Fargo, North Dakota, Fran and I were honored by the congregation when they gave funding for the Lakeside Room in the Mount Carmel Lodge. It is my hope and prayer that Mount Carmel will be like a ship that continues to sail, not drift or lie at anchor, and stay on course delivering the grace-filled cargo of the Word of God.

Chapter Thirteen

JANE SCHUNEMAN, LENORE JESNESS, MICHAEL OVIKIAN

JANE T. SCHUNEMAN

A significant part of the music program at the camp has been the instrumental "Mount Carmel Trio" of violin, cello and piano.

My becoming a part of Mount Carmel started in 1992 when Kay Hoffland, the music director and her daughter Sonja Hinderlie, the program director at Mount Carmel, were looking for a violinist to complete a trio—violin, cello and piano, in order to play for a local wedding. I was honored when they asked me to play with them. We had such a delightful time playing; we decided to continue playing together. Out of that decision the Mount Carmel Trio developed. We have had the joy of planning, arranging and performing a new program every year since that time.

I started playing the violin when I was very young and always played in local events wherever I was living. Violin has been a marvelous inspiration for me. I have never tired of playing and I always give my best.

My husband, Noble, and I moved to a farm that we developed in 1974. It was ten miles southeast of Mount Carmel, near Nelson, Minnesota. Noble died in 2001 which meant I should probably sell the farm and I did. But I have continued to come to Mount Carmel for the summers so our Trio could continue to play.

The whole opportunity of being at this wonderful place and forming the Trio has been a great joy for me. We continue to play for many worship services and concerts during the summer and into the fall. We are finding new ways to expand our music ministry by traveling beyond Mount Carmel, and reaching out to more people in other cities and communities.

I praise and thank the Lord for bringing me into Mount Carmel where I could use my gift of music to glorify my Lord. God's love is ever present as we share the music with our friends and with each other.

LENORE JESNESS, DAUGHTER OF PHIL AND MARIE JESNESS

I met Lenore at a mini-Elderversity during the fall of 2006. She was there as a camper. I saw the name of Jesness on her name tag, and I thought she must be related to Phil Jesness. She said, "Yes, I am one of Phil Jesness's daughters."

There were five children in the Jesness family. The first child died in infancy. The oldest living was Karl, then Lenore, and a brother and sister. She has been coming to Mount Carmel since she was a baby. While growing up in Nelson, Minnesota, she continued to come with her family.

Her mom and dad would come out very often to the camp for Sunday worship and a picnic with their family. It was a favorite place to go. They did not eat in the dinning hall because her dad believed it was reserved for the campers. Besides, they didn't really have the money to eat in the dinning hall. Lenore said she stayed out there as a camper only one time. Otherwise she was a visitor with her mom and dad.

The summers were always beautiful. The family usually walked along the shoreline, looking for a stone to skip in the lake or just have fun listening to the waves and hearing the sounds of water birds. On one part of the shoreline, there was a large rock with a cross on it. Her parents would stand and look at that unique stone, wondering how the cross got there by nature. Then, one spring after a cold winter and lots of ice, the stone was covered up.

Lenore thinks that strong winds blowing the ice up into a huge ridge of ice in the spring moved the stone or tipped it, so that it lost its location forever. Her dad often walked down to the lake and the area where the stone had been when it was first discovered hoping that the stone might someway surface again. But it lies buried in the bank or bottom of the lake.

She said her dad sometimes talked about the tough times at the camp, but they seemed to be hard for everyone. After she finished high school and went out on her own, she did not come to the Mount Carmel for many years. When she came home on her vacations, it was to visit with mom and dad, and return to work. She worked in a laboratory as a medical technologist at a St. Paul, MN hospital.

After her mother died, her father spent more time than ever before at Mount Carmel. He would help out with the fellows doing the maintenance in the camp and whatever job needed to be done. She thinks the Arvid Mattsons who were close friends with her parents, were the custodians who built the house that is called the Jesness House.

She said, "Mount Carmel has had a strong impact on my life and my whole family—more than anyone would ever know or would ever be told. May the Lord continue to use Mount Carmel and to bless the ministry of the Lord Jesus Christ to all who come to this place of Holy Ground!"

MICHAEL OVIKIAN

Michael came to Mount Carmel as a lifeguard in 1959 and again 1960 at the invitation of Pastor Hub Malm. Those two years had an indelible impact on his life. Michael is of Armenian descent and was born and raised in Jerusalem, Israel. He went to school there, loved to study and spoke several languages. He worked summer jobs like any teenager. He became a trained life-guard at the YMCA in the city of Tiberius on the Sea of Galilee.

At age 18, he was working in the world famous King David Hotel where powerful dignitaries came to exchange political opinion. On July 22, 1946, two years before Israel became a nation which was in May, 1948, the hotel was bogie-trapped, bombed and demolished, with over 100 deaths of guests. Michael escaped injury, shielded under a mattress.

He worked for the American General Consulate in Jerusalem for three years before immigrating to America in 1958. He graduated from Augsburg College, cum laude, and began work with the Billy Graham Ministries as the translator of foreign language letters for the worldwide ministry of Billy Graham. In 1991, during the Gulf War, he was assigned as the translator for the King of Jordan.

After his retirement from the Billy Graham Ministries, he became the Mount Carmel Hospitality Director. He is the leader of the Morning Prayer ministry, and a featured speaker. He is a marvelous storyteller and has a magnificent gift of encouragement. He has been present at every Labor Day International Weekend since its beginning in 1986. He has led many trips to his boyhood homeland through Billy Graham and the Mount Carmel tours.

Chapter Fourteen

THE PROCLAIMERS RICHARD SAYTHER

Richard Sayther was the originator of the program for fund raising that became known as The Proclaimers at Mount Carmel. He wrote:

FINANCIAL MANAGEMENT

Mount Carmel was spun off from GVLC in the spring of 1986 when the college closed. The name was changed to Mount Carmel Ministries—encompassing the Bible Camp and the *Psalm of Life* radio program. The name change allowed for future ministry expansion without having to rename the organization whenever additional programs and ministries were added. In the fall of 1986, there was an appeal to friends to raise some funds to help pay for capital expenses and for some of the debt incurred in the transfer of the ownership.

I became involved with Mount Carmel in 1987 right after this first attempt to raise money. Immediately our objectives were to build a development department to generate on-going support for the operations, and to build a development program to gather gifts throughout the coming years. The annual fund was the first focus. Annual fund is described as "annual recurring gifts for annual recurring needs." So rather than focus on debt reduction, the plan was to build programs that would bring in gifts for operations. The Proclaimers was the key program within the annual fund.

I think, Johan Hinderlie originated the name Proclaimer based on a Scripture from 1 Corinthians 9:14, "...*The Lord commanded that those who proclaim the*

Gospel should get their living by the Gospel." (NASV) Originally, Proclaimers were a giving club wherein people who gave $100 or more during a calendar year were members of Proclaimers for that year.

The entry membership level of Proclaimers was increased later to $200 or more in a calendar year. This system continues to this day. Such giving clubs are typical of successful annual funds. Right from the beginning of building the development program, concern was expressed about the ownership of Mount Carmel Ministries. Initially, and at the time the development program was beginning, the Board of Trustees was self-perpetuating—that is, the board members elected other board members. There was no ownership of the ministry beyond the board itself. Obviously this was neither good nor right.

The question of ownership was important to friends and donors who wanted to be sure the ministry was owned by enough people to assure its future and not be dependent entirely upon the current board and staff. After studying various ways of establishing ownership, such as an association of congregations, the board decided to change the constitution so that individuals who gave leadership and financial support would be the owners of Mount Carmel Ministries. The constitution allowed that if a person (or couple) were members in a given year, they were voting members at the next year's annual meeting. Two safeguards—the nominating committee and the election of the Board of Directors were built in so that no outside group could ever deviously, illegally or unethically gain direction or control or ownership of the camp and property.

Early on there were "annual meetings" every week in the summer so guests would know how the ministry was operating and what the plans were for the future. After the change of ownership to Proclaimers, one annual meeting was scheduled for the purpose of electing the members of the board.

Today, the Proclaimers serve a valuable function in the life of Mount Carmel. Not only are they the primary system for encouraging, asking for pledges and acknowledging gifts from individuals to the annual fund, these

Proclaimers also form the body of people who truly own and operate the ministry. It is the Proclaimers who become generous donors to the capital projects and to the Endowment Fund. And, it is the Proclaimers who safeguard the ownership of the property of Mount Carmel Ministries. The Proclaimers have become the heart and soul and spirit of Mount Carmel Ministries.

In summary, Proclaimers are the owners of Mount Carmel Ministries who support the proclamation of the Gospel in such a way that the grace of our Lord Jesus Christ is experienced, and lives are transformed. The Proclaimers elect the Board of Trustees, and help Mount Carmel with their gifts, participation and prayers.

In a Report on the Building Blessings Appeal to the Mount Carmel Annual Meeting on May 13, 2006, Richard who is Managing Partner, at Gronlund Sayther Brunkow GSB, wrote, "I am especially pleased to see once again the generous response of people who care so deeply about the ministry. Since 1987 I have been privileged to be associated with Mount Carmel both as an advisor and also as a member of Proclaimers and donor to capital appeals. Like you, I consider this ministry to be vital to people and to the church...Together as we tell the story, lift up the ministry and the appeal in prayer, and confidently invite each other to give as the Lord has given to us, the goal will be reached."

Chapter Fifteen

MEMBERS OF THE BOARD OF DIRECTORS, AND BISHOP JOHN BEEM

I suggested to Pastor John Beem, the retired Bishop of the Northwest Synod of Wisconsin of The Evangelical Lutheran Church in America, and members of the Board that they dream about the future—the next 70 years for Mount Carmel. What do they envision? How might the camp continue to proclaim the Gospel simply and to the larger community? Who knows how the Lord will use Mount Carmel, but it is important for the leadership to dream. John wrote:

JESUS ONLY, OUR TRUE FOCUS

The next 70 years will remain as it has been these past years with "Jesus Only" as our true focus. *"Suddenly when they looked around, they saw no one with them any more, but Jesus only."* Mark 9: 8, NRSV.

We believe that throughout the coming years, God will provide leaders, teachers, and counselors who will continue to draw individuals to more fully understand God's grace and love in their lives. The true focus must remain, "Jesus Only." The Psalmist declares, *"One generation shall laud your works to another, and shall declare your mighty acts."* Psalm 145:4 NRSV. We dare to believe that our God will be faithful to coming generations and will continue to raise up leaders, as well as those who will support this ministry with attendance and their gifts in order to maintain a unique opportunity for reaching people with the good news of Christ the Lord.

Jesus said, *"For every one who asks receives, and everyone who searches finds, and for everyone who knocks, the door will be opened."* Luke 11:10, NRSV. This will continue to be the emphasis for the next 70 years at Mount Carmel. It will be a place where people dare to ask questions, while seeking answers to a deeper relationship with Jesus Christ. They will knock on many doors which need to be opened by the power of the Holy Spirit for themselves as individuals and for the benefit of the church and society.

Mount Carmel will stay focused on Jesus through a concentrated study of the Bible—the Word of God. We believe the ministry with the aid of modern technology will offer classes taught by professors and leaders at institutions and centers hundreds of miles from our actual facilities. Participants and leaders alike will need to be of one mind and one Spirit while exploring the many faceted aspects of life in this century.

The summers and the winters, too, will continue to be a blessing for families in their growth in grace, but we also believe the ministry will expand as the ministry reaches out to serve the community and church at large with caregivers and resource leaders. Mount Carmel's independence will be a wonderful asset in the ecumenical endeavors of the future while staying true to its roots of Lutheranism which was vital to the founding leaders.

We truly believe the best years are ahead for Mount Carmel Ministries. New facilities will offer opportunities for study and worship, and for building up the whole body of Christ. We stand on the threshold of an exciting opportunity for the generations to come.

Our vision is likely to be exciting as we dream, pray a lot, and reveal dreams for the next 70 years of our ministries. We hope you will forward those dreams in the days and years to come to the Board of Trustees.

WHAT WILL IT BE?

On the 140th birthday—years 1938 to 2078, the question is: "What will Mount Carmel be like 70 years from now—the year 2078 when it celebrates the 140th anniversary of this ministry?" The answer is: "Who knows but the

LORD, the God Almighty?" Nevertheless, we dare to posit certain things will be true about Mount Carmel Ministries and its properties. Mount Carmel will:

1. Continue as a center for family camping as one of many venues offered on its campus. Retreat ministries will escalate, affording Mount Carmel to address a growing assortment of human needs in the name of Jesus.

2. Become a strong fixture in the greater Alexandria area, proudly supported by the community for the cultural events and healing ministries.

3. Be a community. Our campus will include a retirement center, low income apartment housing for seniors, an assisted living complex, and a condominium village.

4. Become a congregation. On-site residents could become members.

The Proclaimers would be associate members. Members will be committed to a vibrant missional ministry with continuing connections in the World Mission Prayer League and to Slovakia. The population north of Alexandria will continue to be a fertile challenge for evangelistic outreach. Our budget will be built around 50% of all income being used for benevolent causes.

5. Have a resident pastor well grounded in Lutheran orthodox theology in the spirit of the Lutheran Bible Institute. Such a theological posture will be a welcome resource for those seeking spiritual stability and a devotional life to sustain them in their ministries. A growing staff will be called by this expanding parish, but the staff will be limited by the resourceful use of the time and talents of the community.

6. Be a major learning center, both experiential and academic. By 2080 cultural assimilation into the life of the Church, faith diversity, and other assaults on the Gospel will place Mount Carmel in the role of being a much sought after place for renewal of home, family, and church complete with sound theological training of both lay and clergy as well as training in a solid devotional base for living in Jesus.

7. Be recognized as a center for preserving the traditional Reformation articulation of the authority of the Word. The demand for such a min-

istry will empower Mount Carmel to become a hub throughout the ecumenical circle for a consortium of nation wide satellite centers.

8. Become a player in facilitating Lutheran unity between current denominational separations.

9. Experience increased financial support beyond those generated by Proclaimers from expanded campus revenues, from the campus congregational residential facilities, and from congregations that endorse the theological base of our ministries which lead to the renewal of Christianity.

10. Become a much larger campus having purchased and developed land across Mount Carmel Drive and Douglas County Road number 11.

We invite you to dream for the future. Dream with us! Forward them to the Board of Trustees of Mount Carmel Ministries. One thing, however, is for certain. Mount Carmel will depend on the power of the Holy Spirit to guide and direct our ministries in the next seventy years. To Him be the glory!

Written by Retired Bishop John Beem and Rev. Dr. Lloyd Wallace with ideas gleaned from current and past members of the Board of Trustees and from a wide assortment of friends of Mount Carmel. The content of this chapter does not speak for the Board of Trustees individually or corporately.

Chapter Sixteen

Author's Observations
Orval Kenneth Moren

Mount Carmel Ministries

Mount Carmel, which I have previously called—a Bible Camp, is part of Mount Carmel Ministries. As you read, you noticed there are several ministries and the Camp is one of them. We don't call the facility a "camp" any longer. We describe it as a Renewal Center. It is really a center for relaxing, for study, for play, for spiritual renewal of relationship with the Lord Jesus Christ, and with like-minded friends.

As you have read the through *The Mount Carmel Story*, you have discovered that the remembrances of how and why Mount Carmel Ministries came into being are varied with each person. There is a good explanation in the 1998 Annual Report.

"In 1985, following the closing of Golden Valley Lutheran College, the land was faced with a new challenge. The parent organization, The Lutheran Bible Institute could no longer carry this mission. To continue the summer teaching ministry, there would need to be a new organization. People who believed in the place and its legacy of ministry joined to create a new ministry called Mount Carmel Ministries. In order to purchase the property, money was needed to satisfy the debt on the land. By 1987, Mount Carmel Ministries had raised enough money to cover the down payment for the land and its buildings. These were purchased from The Lutheran Bible Institute of Minneapolis for the sum of the debt on Mount Carmel, $720,000. In 1992, $420,000 of the debt was paid off and by 1997; the $300,000 balance had been satisfied."

THE ORIGINAL BOARD

The original Board of Mount Carmel Ministries was elected on August 9, 1986. Elected were: Norman Anderson, Ernest Bakken, Charles Blastervold, Neil Ericksmoen, Johan Hinderlie, Sonja Hinderlie, Irene Myhro, Jim Nelson, Wally Ness, Helen Savage, and Linda Simpson.

After formation, the Board met every month—September, October, November, and December in an attempt to begin to establish financial stability prior to year end. The Board set short and long term goals for the future and continuing of Mount Carmel Ministries.

NINE SHORT TERM GOALS WERE SET

1. Secure needed annual pledges

2. Operate Mount Carmel at a profit

3. Build interest for Mount Carmel in the Alexandria area

4. Equip more cabins with shower and rest room facilities

5. Construct a public rest room in a central location

6. Clear the woods of trees and shrubs to improve accessibility and create hiking trails

7. Improve the campsites

8. Improve the Youth Chapel and Center

9. Organize Mount Carmel's 50th anniversary celebration for 1988

FOUR LONG TERM GOALS WERE DETERMINED

1. Create a facility for year-round ministry

2. Design property and programming to serve community needs of individual churches

3. Equip facility to meet needs of handicapped individuals

4. Renovate the kitchen facility

PROPERTY SECURED

The first issue of *The Messenger* Volume 1, No.1 was printed and sent out in January 1987. The head line declared, "Mount Carmel Ministries Secures Property."

The article stated that the Board had determined to cash the checks from donations, and that the property be purchased. Terms had been arranged with the Golden Valley Bank, and word was being waited from the Board of Trustees of The American Lutheran Church concerning the outstanding loan they had with Mount Carmel.

The second issue of *The Messenger* Volume 1, No.2, April, 1987, carried the headline, "Mount Carmel Makes History." The back cover states that *The Messenger* will be issued January 15, April 15, and September 15. The editor was Irene Myhro. The editor wrote this as the featured front page article.

"History was made as the Mount Carmel property was transferred to Mount Carmel Ministries. Charles Blastervold, chairman of the Mt. Carmel Board and Sonja Hinderlie, president of Mount Carmel Ministries, signed the documents on March 17th, 1987.

For 49 years the property of Mount Carmel was owned by The Lutheran Bible Institute. Because of encumbrances on the property due to the closing of Golden Valley Lutheran College, it seemed important to preserve this ministry in any way possible. After an intensive fund drive last fall, $150,000 was raised to begin negotiations with the creditors. On December 31, 1986, a purchase agreement was signed with the Golden Valley Bank for $420,000. Transfer of ownership to Mount Carmel Ministries is a significant change for Mount Carmel since the operation had been subsidized by the LBI for so many years. Thanks to the dedication of those who have believed in this ministry over the years and financially took a step of faith, the property and ministry is secured for another half century!"

On page 9 of this 2nd issue of *The Messenger* was the Board Report. I am quoting excerpts from the Report. "The last Board meeting was held…on March 17, 1987. Linda Simpson resigned from the Board as she is expecting a baby. Larry Beckman will take over her duties as secretary to fill out the term… Total pledges are currently $22,000 per year for 5 years. Closing on the property took place on March 17, 1987 at 1:30 p.m. at the Golden Valley Bank… Staffing duties and salaries were discussed and assigned. Ruby and Les Larsen decided not to return this summer (for maintenance and custodial). The Director will be paid April 1 through September 30. The President will be paid for building up the ministry on an annual basis. The next Meeting is April 25, 1987…" On page 10, the Financial Report for August 1, 1986 through March 31, 1987 was given. The balance on hand at 3/31/87 was $72,521.15.

The Report stated, "PRAISE THE LORD! God works in a mysterious way His wonders to perform as pledges are coming in. Already, $22,000 has been pledged per year for 5 years. At least $31,000 per year is the necessary goal so that monthly payments can be met on the Mount Carmel property. For the first two years the pledge of $31,000 pays the interest only. In the third year interest payment plus payment of the principal commences. Our prayer is that payments on principal can start sooner as we exceed the $31,000 pledged per year. The 5 year pledge period is January 1, 1987 through December 31, 1991. Keeping current on pledge amounts is important so we can fulfill commitments that the Lord has placed on us…"

At the time, March 1987, the President of the Mount Carmel Board of Directors was Charles Blastervold. The Director of Mount Carmel Ministries was Johan Hinderlie, and the President of the Mount Carmel Ministries was

Sonja Hinderlie. Johan could not be the president because he was still the President of Lutheran Bible Institute, even though Golden Valley Lutheran College was closed.

You have read the fascinating and nearly miraculous story of the challenge that Dr. Courtland Agre gave to the guests and supporters, and Proclaimers. As I researched and interviewed sources for my writing, in the spring of 2006, I asked Ellen Agre, the widow of Dr. Courtland Agre, if she remembered this happening. She replied to me, "Oh yes, I remember it well. I thought it was a significant gift of money. But once Court had made up his mind, he didn't change. He loved Mount Carmel. He loved to go alone and spend his time painting the buildings. Because of his cancer, he knew his days were numbered. The money was actually his personal money."

On page 3 of the April 1987 issue of *The Messenger*, Johan, as the new camp director laid out a plan to invite others. He wrote, "Just as with your church, most people come to Mount Carmel at the invitation of someone they trust. Your message to your vacation-planning friends and relatives is important to Mount Carmel's registrations. Paint a picture of your memories of Mount Carmel. In this way your friend can fit herself or himself into your picture. A friend is more willing to do this after he or she knows you have heard and sympathized with their story.

He continued, "Finally, remember that the Spirit of God breathes Mount Carmel's unique life together. He creates the sense of belonging hand peace with God that has been a wonderful benefit of our Bible centered ministry. Your conversation can draw people to this place of grace but only God will meet them at their point-of-need to give them the free vacation rest they need now that can last eternally."

In August, 18 and 19, 1987, the schedule was changed so that two groups of seniors could come for a daylong event. Four key persons were available for these groups: Marva Dawn from Notre Dame University, Janet and Kent Hill with music from Elmira, New York, and Johan who at that time was the *Psalm of Life* radio pastor. It was the forerunner of the program, which eventually became the weeks of Elderversity in August and September.

BASIC HISTORICAL OUTLINE OF THE HISTORY OF THE LUTHERAN BIBLE INSTITUTE

The Bible Banner, Volume 1, Number 2, in March, 1920 had a report from Pastor Samuel Miller to the Board of Directors of The Lutheran Bible Institute. The report says, "The Lutheran Bible Institute began to exist as a working institution on the evening of the 16th of September (1919), when an opening exercise was held at First Lutheran Church, St. Paul, (MN). At this service, Pastor G.N. Anderson made an address in which he publicly presented me with the office of Dean. I responded with an address in which I attempted to present the objects and aims of the new movement. The next day, September 17th, the school actually began to function."

The school was established in 1919 with classes at First Lutheran Church in St. Paul, and then at the Hamline Seminary. Some classes in the evening were held at Messiah Lutheran Church in Minneapolis, Minnesota. Classes began in fall of 1929 at the newly constructed building at 1619 Portland, downtown Minneapolis, Minnesota.

From the very beginning plans were laid for a summer school. In his report, Dean Miller said, "The Board should soon decide definitely in the matter of a Summer School." The report states, they looked at Gustavus Adolphus College in St. Peter. They surveyed the Inner Mission property at Lake Johanna for a tent colony. They looked at the Old People's Home area in Chisago City. A property such as Mount Carmel was in the minds of the leadership of the Lutheran Bible Institute from its birth.

In 1961, LBI moved to a new campus in Golden Valley. In 1967, the LBI as a school became the Golden Valley Lutheran College under the umbrella of The Lutheran Bible Institute with 225 students. By the fall of 1978, enrollment was 590 students. However, in 1984, enrollment decreased to 429.

In April of 1985, the Board of Regents decided the school would not open in the fall in September, so that May 24, 1985 marked the final Commencement for the GVLC and LBI. During the 66 year period—1919 through May 1985, 19,422 persons are considered alumni.

THE LUTHERAN BIBLE INSTITUTE FOUNDATIONS

As I searched for the origins and the foundations of Mount Carmel, I came upon the foundations that had been laid for the Lutheran Bible Institute. Mount Carmel is today what it is because of the beginnings it has had in the first and second meetings of the Lutheran Bible Institute. From the beginning, a retreat location set apart for study of the Scriptures, and prayer with meaningful worship was in the plans of the founder and the board of directors.

In the spring of 1972, Dr. Miller brought a greeting to the students and faculty at the Lutheran Bible Institute in Los Angeles. Dr. Miller told the audience in his greeting that he was now 80 years old. His plea to them was that they would continue to study the Word of God, and determine what the Lord has for them. "I still believe," he said, "that the greatest youth movement is that young people dedicate their lives to live for Jesus and to the glory of his name." We will read just a short part of the Greeting for his insights.

"Greetings…It is now over 52 years since we began the Lutheran Bible Institute and the Bible Study Movement. We thank God that it has continued down through the years…I rejoice greatly, that you are continuing in the same way that we began, with a positive and affirmative study of the Word of God, encouraging young people especially, to set aside a year or even two years of their lives to really let God speak to them through His Holy Word…To permit the Word of God speak to us and reveal to us the Lord Jesus Christ, so that we might experience His call to us and to plan our lives according to His will and for His glory.

I am now an old man, having gone past my 80 years (I will be 81 this next summer) and haven't found any reason to change the aim and purpose with which we began the work of the Lutheran Bible Institute. I still believe that is the greatest kind of youth movement there ever can be in our land or in the world that young people dedicated their lives to live for Jesus, and the glory of His name."

Pastor Maynard A. Force, president of the Bible School in California interviewed Dr. Miller in Miller's home in what he called "his doghouse" which was his office. The full original tape of the greeting and interview by Pastor Force is available from the Mount Carmel Library. The first question from Pastor Force centered on Miller's beginning of the School in 1919.

Dr. Miller told Maynard that he was at that time, the Pastor of Messiah Lutheran Church of the Augustana Synod in Minneapolis. There was an awakening among some of the pastors and young people. They wanted to study the Bible. They could take Bible courses in the various colleges of the church, but most indicated they wanted a school that specialized only in Bible Study.

Miller resigned from the Messiah Lutheran Church in order to begin the Bible School. It would be called the Lutheran Bible Institute. The school began in the basement of First Lutheran Church in St. Paul, where George Anderson was pastor. Pr. Anderson had married Annette Elmquist who had experience in a non-Lutheran Bible School, and had been one of Dr. Miller's students and supporters. By the end of the first year—1920, there were twenty students. Two years later, ten students graduated with a diploma.

From the beginning, Dr. Miller had other part-time helpers and teachers. Pastor A.B. (Alfred Bertil) Anderson of the Norwegian Lutheran Church had begun a Bible School in Spokane, Washington. He was called to join the Lutheran Bible Institute in 1922 as a full-time teacher along with Dr. Miller.

After coming, he began to lose his good health, and by 1930 he became handicapped. He taught from a wheelchair where he probably was more powerful than he had been on his two feet. He was a great soul winner.

The third man called to the LBI was Dr. C. J. (Carl Johan) Sodergren who came on a part-time basis. The next full-time teacher was Odd J. Gornitzka who became the Dean of the School.

When the school moved from St. Paul to Minneapolis in 1929 into the new building, one of the reasons for moving was the prevailing idea that Minneapolis was stronger Lutheran and St. Paul was more Roman Catholic. There seemed to be more interest and more opportunity in the Minneapolis community. The school moved to downtown Minneapolis because it was in the heart of the city where they wanted to be. Not out in the country!

A lot was found and bought for $15, 000 on Portland Avenue. The school had $50,000 to start the building, and the project was estimated to cost $250,000 total. The year was 1928 and 1929. The $50,000 was in bonds, and drawing interest. Dr. Miller told Pastor Force that he was concerned about the economy at that time. He went to the bank, withdrew the monies and paid the contractor in advance during the summer of 1929. Happily and with the Lord's blessing, no payment was ever missed in paying for the construction of the building.

The school sessions began in the fall of 1929 before the building was completed. There was no tuition for any student, boy or girl. There was a small registration fee and the cost of room and board for the girls who stayed in the school dormitory. Dr. Miller remembered the classes began with about 100 students that fall of 1929. In 1948, the 1000th student received a graduating diploma.

Dr. Miller related to Pastor Force that some heartache and sadness for him and the school came from students who debated the Word of God and challenged their faith in the Lord Jesus. There was sadness for those students who left the faith and fell into sin.

There was also a hardship with students from various nationalistic backgrounds for many different reasons. Especially this was true of Norwegian and Swedes, and those of German background, but the blending of the students helped to merge the entire Lutheran church into the Lutheran community in the years to come.

The summer Bible Camps were especially used for the Lord to bring about changed lives among the young people. Pastor Force asked Dr. Miller if he thought that the Lutheran Bible Institute movement was the first to start summer camps. Dr. Miller responded that he thought that was true. Dr. Miller went on to say, that the first camp began in June of 1921 at Lake Independence, just west of Minneapolis.

He was courting his wife to be, Helene Forsberg, whom he married in 1914 during those camping days. The owners of the facilities at Lake Independence said they would build for the camp. But, Dr. Miller decided to find his own place because the camp there was not feeding the school with students. There were too many other kinds of groups of young people there. Dr. Miller began looking around and rented a camp near Alexandria. Then in 1938, the land near Lake Carlos, a few miles north and west of Alexandria, Minnesota, was purchased that would become Mount Carmel.

An article in *The Bible Banner* by Rev. Emory Johnson of Buhl, Minnesota describes the location and the work as it progressed.

"Mount Carmel is on a high promontory, on the north shore of Lake Carlos. There is half a mile of excellent beach, and the water is clean. Rising to a height of thirty feet above the lake, the grounds command an inspiring view of the lake, which is about seven miles long. The south wind is cool at Mount Carmel, because of its long sweep over the miles of water. The lake is deep and therefore cool.

The twin knolls on Mount Carmel have been fittingly utilized for the main buildings, the auditorium, which can accommodate 600 worshippers, and the spacious dining hall, which also includes an inviting lobby and refreshment center. The prominent feature of the lobby is the cobble-stone fireplace which will help to brighten and cheer evenings that may be cool.

Cabins and housekeeping cottages, thirty-eight in number, have been built among the trees and along the brow of the hill east of the main buildings. These will accommodate 134 guests. In three months the place was transformed from a rock-infested, stump-covered hillside farm to an attractive, practical, and well-equipped summer home, with roads, gravel walks, flower beds and window boxes, electric lights, running water, luxurious beds and other facilities. The beds deserve special mention for usually one does not expect to find coil springs and inner-spring mattresses at a summer camp, except perhaps at the swankiest and costliest resorts.

A crew of workers has been busy at Mount Carmel since April. The concrete foundations for the buildings required the digging of miles of trenches. Another mile of digging was needed for water pipes leading from the pressure tank to the various buildings. And to connect up a mile of pipe is no small task. Where the auditorium now stands the workmen found thirty-three large stumps which had to be removed before construction could be begun. Though much work yet remains to be done, Mount Carmel was ready to receive guests on the day announced for its opening. On July 2 the doors were opened, and the first to register was a family from Spokane, Washington.

Dr. Miller wrote poetry. He was a composer of music for his poetic hymns. The words of the song, "Jesus Only", appeared in *The Bible Banner,* Volume 1, and Number 4 in July, 1920. In Volume 1, and Number 5, the music appeared on the back page.

Jesus only on the mountain, Jesus only on the sea,
Jesus only in the valley, There in dark Gethsemane.
Jesus only to Golgotha, Jesus only on the cross,
Jesus only in all suffering, All things else are empty dross.

Jesus only in life's evening, Jesus only gives me rest,
Jesus only can support me, When the sun sinks in the west.
Jesus only in the morning, Of the vast eternity,
There revealed in glorious, In the home He won for me.

Pastor Miller wrote on the top of the original manuscript, the words of the disciples who were with Jesus on the Mount of Transfiguration in Matthew 17:8, *"And lifting up their eyes, they saw no one else, save Jesus only."* What he felt and what inspired him about their experience, we don't know. The hymn is sung often at Mount Carmel. A cross flower garden with "Jesus Only" which has been moved several times as new buildings and roads have come into being is a constant reminder of the hymn.

Samuel Martin Miller was born on August 26, 1890 in Lowell, Massachusetts to Anders P. Miller and Julia Linderith. He graduated from Upsala College, with a Bachelor of Arts degree in 1910, and from Augustana Seminary with a Bachelor of Divinity in 1913 and was ordained June 15, 1913. His first Call was to Trinity Lutheran in Moline, Illinois 1913-1916. Dr. Miller died on February 26, 1975. The information in this paragraph is available in The Augustana Ministerium, 1850-1962 at Luther Theological Seminary, 2481 Como Avenue, St. Paul, Minnesota.

THE LEGACY WE INHERITED WE TAKE WITH US

Mount Carmel Ministries exists today only because there was a beginning through a Bible School. I believe it would be wise for us to remember our roots. Therefore, I have gleaned out some essentials of our heritage from the LBI.

The Bible Banner, Volume I. Number 2, March, 1920 on the front page lists the Principles, Purposes and Plans of the Lutheran Bible Institute.

PRINCIPLES

The Lutheran Bible Institute stands for:

The Bible as the inspired Word of God;

The whole body of Doctrine and Principles of Conduct of the Lutheran Church, as contained in the Confessional Writings of said Church, feeling that the denials of the day demand an emphasis on the following Lutheran and Bible doctrines;

The Deity of the virgin-born Jesus Christ,

Christ's victorious blood-atonement,

Christ's bodily resurrection and ascension and His imminent return in glory,

Justification by faith alone,

The Word, Baptism and Lord's Supper as the only means of grace,

Good Works as fruits of a living faith.

However, it is not in the Principles of the Lutheran Bible Institute to make a special hobby of any one particular doctrine but to teach the full Gospel from the whole Word of God.

PURPOSES

The Lutheran Bible Institute purposes, God Willing,

To continually emphasize the need of systematic, intensive Bible study,

To present methods and directions for Bible study,

To be a power-house of life from the Word studied under prayer,

To seek thru prayer and Bible study to create a spiritual atmosphere in the School,

To implant the Living Word in the hearts and lives of the students,

To train Bible Teachers,

To train lay workers for the foreign mission fields,

To train lay workers for the inner mission fields,

To train lay workers for the home churches,

To send out students with a passion for souls,

To send out students who will dare to do and die for Jesus,

To seek to know the will of God and act accordingly,

To prove that God still answers prayer,

To be a truly Lutheran Bible School.

PLANS

The Lutheran Bible Institute plans, God Willing,

To develop a strong Lutheran Bible School Centre in the Northwest,

To develop three courses in the Day School,

Christian Workers Course, one year,

Bible Teachers course, two years,

Missionary Course, two years,

To conduct a short-term Summer Bible School,

To develop extension departments wherever opportunity is afforded,

To seek no official aid or connection with any church, synod or conference,

To seek to gain and deserve the confidence and moral support of all Lutheran Bodies,

To especially so seek to pray, purpose and plan as to gain the confidence and financial support of all earnest Christians in all Lutheran Bodies,

To present the needs of the movement wherever freely permitted,

To let the Spirit of God do all the soliciting,

To depend for all things entirely upon God's answer to prayer,

To ask God for an Establishment Fund of a Hundred Thousand Dollars.

To ask God for a hundred friends who will each pray for One Thousand Dollars.

To ask God for teachers and students,

To ask God for faith to believe in His promise of answered prayer.

OBSERVATION

I noticed that the Summer Bible School idea was number three in the list of priorities. From the very beginning, a summer school was planned. *The Bible Banner*, Volume I, Number 3, May, 1920 on the front page, has a large advertisement: SUMMER VACATION BIBLE SCHOOL, and the place listed is beautiful Lake Independence, Maple Plain, Minnesota. From the first full summer, there has been a place such as a Mount Carmel.

THE BIBLE BANNER

The Bible Banner, Volume I. Number 2, March, 1920, page 3 had a column describing the origins of **The Bible Banner**. Part of the article reads,

"In accordance with a decision of the Board, the Executive Committee proceeded with the publication of a Bulletin to represent the affairs of the school and to be a medium for suggesting helps for Bible study. We decided to issue it bi-monthly. We named it "The Bible Banner." The first issue was dated January 1ˢᵗ…The paper will contain devotional material, news about the school, a students department and Bible studies. Three more issues will contain eight studies each in the Book of Acts along the line of those already published. This question and suggestion method of Bible study seems to be a new departure in our Lutheran Church…."

In the next issue—number 3, of *The Bible Banner*, there were several letters from pastors and lay people that were printed about the great help the Bible studies had been to some pastors and youth. The Bible studies made an immediate impact and were well received from the first and second issues.

One of the letters from Dr. Philip Andreen said, "I wish to thank you for copy of *The Bible Banner*. I hope you will send me the paper regularly. I shall also with my young people go thru Acts this winter and spring. Your lesson will give me great help. God bless you in your noble work."

Three editors are named: Dean S. M. Miller, Editor in Chief; Pastor Geo. N. Anderson and Mrs. Geo. N. Anderson, Assistant Editors. Since the article is part of the Deans' Report, maybe we can assume the naming of *The Bible Banner* and the Scriptures comes from Pastor Miller himself. The name for *The Bible Banner* magazine came from Psalm 60: 4, *"Thou hast given a banner to them that fear Thee, that it may be displayed because of the truth."* And from the Canticle 2:4, "His banner over me was love."

MOUNT CARMEL OWNERSHIP

Mount Carmel is owned by the Proclaimers who support the proclamation of the gospel in such a way that the grace of our Lord Jesus Christ is experienced and lives are transformed. Proclaimers elect the Board of Trustees and help Mount Carmel with their gifts, participation and prayers.

Richard Sayther's chapter 14 presents the complete story of financial management and ownership.

Mount Carmel Ministries is a 501c (3) non-profit, Minnesota corporation whose members are individuals and congregations who have given annual financial support to the ministry of $200.00 or more each year. Mount Carmel is an outdoor ministry affiliated with the Evangelical Lutheran Church in America. Mount Carmel is a teaching ministry designed to strengthen the faith of individual and families.

A volunteer Board of Trustees, elected by the membership at the annual meeting, provides financial and policy oversight for the future of the organization. The Board of Trustees hires an Executive Director who has responsibility for the day-to-day management of the organization.

The Proclaimer membership has grown to more than 560 individuals, families, churches and organizations in the year 2007. Each Proclaimer has given $200 or more to the Annual Fund. They gave collectively a total of $367,524 dollars in the year 2006. Thrivent Financial for Lutheran's Giving Plus program has helped enormously. We want to thank sincerely everyone who participated in the Proclaimers program.

WHO IS MOUNT CARMEL AND IT'S MINISTRIES?

The answer to the question is really quite simple. It is a community. It is people. An article in *The Messenger*, which is the official newsletter of Mount Carmel Ministries in the winter of 2005, written by Sonja Hinderlie beautifully tells us who Mount Carmel is. "Mount Carmel is a Christ-centered community with fellowship for all ages where the gospel is experienced. The mission of Mount Carmel Ministries is to foster spiritual growth in Jesus Christ by applying the Bible to daily life." The **vision** of Mount Carmel Ministries is to transform lives through "Jesus Only." The **purpose** of Mount Carmel is to equip people for service and to enable equipped-people to share the gospel in order to proclaim the name of Jesus.

Located on pristine Lake Carlos, Mount Carmel was established in Alexandria, Minnesota in 1938 as a place for families, adults and youth to receive renewal from the study of the Word of God. Since its humble beginning it has grown to include: thirty family size cabins and cozy cottages; ten campsites for summer and fall programs; and a spacious lodge providing year-around accommodations which make winter and spring retreats possible and in 2008 a new Learning Center which houses the new Chapel.

Mount Carmel Ministries has grown from the legacy of a retreat center only and extends beyond its borders in many ways. Bible study programs taught by a vibrant faculty from places near and far equip participants with skills for teaching and sharing in local congregations. The music ministry has been at the core for many years. Prayer and healing retreats bring transformation and life-changing power into people's lives. This power propels people into a hurting world as ministers of God's grace and compassion. Programs provided by this ministry are taken into congregations throughout the country. A simple devotional book, *Daily Texts*, is produced annually, which expands the Mount Carmel experience to the whole world.

Sonja interviewed Dr. Fred Townsend in an article in *The Messenger* in the winter of 2005. He is Chair of the Mount Carmel Board of Directors. The interview focused on the Master Plan, which has been developed over months of planning. Several significant decisions have been made that directly change the direction of the future of this Adult and Family Renewal Center. This is a summary of that article.

Several Task forces had been meeting to look toward the future. Surveys among the summer guests and the Proclaimers had been taken and processed. The one large question which the task force dealt with was whether to have a year long schedule of the camp or not. The decision was made, at that time, to hold a six month schedule, from May through October. That decision cleared the air and gave focus for new direction in the future.

The first phase in the master plan concerns the facilities. The question has been: Should the Miller Chapel be replaced or renovated, and should it be winterized? With a six month season, there would be no need to have a winterized Miller Chapel, and the decision was made to remodel it. However, upon further review and investigation into the cost of re-construction, this decision was reversed. A new Miller Chapel would be built. That happened during the winter of 2007 and 2008.

In the first phase planning, 24 cabins also will be upgraded and remodeled, but not winterized. There will be new windows, refinished floors, with new plumbing and lighting. Some of the housekeeping cabins will be moved. Others will be removed to make way for some new construction and roads. This has been accomplished by 2008.

The second phase will involve developing a camping center, activity center for youth and fixing up the waterfront. The last phase will be building a new chapel and other winterized lodging. This phase was accelerated because of the great response in the Building Blessings financial campaign, and a most favorable bid for construction of the Learning Center in the winter of 2007-2008.

How were these decisions by the board reached? The following is a long quote from Dr. Townsend,

"After the brainstorming event at the end of January in 2004, we worked with a consultant named Anne Hunter. She really helped us organize our thinking and establish our vision and mission. It was a great way to start and focus on our common ideas for the strategic plan. Then we began the work with Kathleen Trotter, our master planner. She helped us analyze the land use, facilities, and finances of current and projected projects. She also helped get the guest surveys prepared and interpreted."

Dr. Townsend continued as he outlined the mission of Mount Carmel,

"We see the need for Mount Carmel to fill the niche of a spiritual training and education center for congregations, pastors, young people, lay leaders, families—year around. Mount Carmel has had the mission of "holding forth the Word of Life" in its tradition. Teaching the Bible and applying it to everyday life is the key thread that comes from the past and carries us into the future. This board has taken this very seriously and as a result has not wanted to act too hastily on all of these decisions without weighing this strong identity of "Jesus Only". It feels we are more empowered as a board to take the needed steps with confidence as we are "on the same page."

As you read you soon realize that decisions were made and then reversed. New decisions were made and then reversed again. As the board received new information on possible estimated costs, on reports from structural engineers, and as plans for the future developed, new strategies for ministry developed. The board and the leadership must be credited with willingness to listen and respond as they prayed through options and decisions.

Names of Mount Carmel Preachers, Teachers and Leaders

A. B. (Alfred Bertil) Anderson, preacher and teacher

Courtland Agre, wife Ellen, chemist and professor

Diogenes Allen, teacher and professor

John Beem, bishop retired and board member

Anchor Samuel Berg, preacher and teacher

James (Jim) Richard Bjorge, preacher and teacher

John Robert Bjorge, preacher and teacher

Roy Bloomquist, wife Marjorie, camp director

Marva Dawn, teacher and professor

Wilson Blaine Fagerberg, preacher and teacher

Maynard Alfred Force, preacher and teacher

Garcia Grindal, teacher and professor

C.O. Grundland, preacher and teacher

Odd J. Gornitzka, preacher and teacher

Oscar C. Hanson, preacher, teacher and president

Johan Hinderlie, wife Sonja, camp director

Sonja Hinderlie, husband Johan, camp programs

Karla Holterman, teacher

Kay Hoffland, husband Richard, music ministry

Edna Hong, teacher

Karla Holterman, teacher

Philip Jesness, wife Marguerite, carpenter

E.W. Klawitter, speaker, *Psalm of Life*

A. W. (Arthur Wilhelm) Knock, teacher

Luther Lerseth, wife Jean, camp director

Herbert and Edna Loddigs, preacher and teacher

Erman Kornelius Lunder, preacher teacher

Samuel Martin Miller, wife Helene Forsberg, founder

Rene (Fredin) Moen, husband Jon, business manager

Herbert (Hub) Emil Malm, wife Evelyn, camp director

Irene Myhro, husband Norman, historian and board member

Alvar Nelson, business manager

Marvin and Theresa Nysetvold, assistant director

Bernt Christian Opsal, wife Shirley, preacher and president

Jim Otterness, preacher and teacher

Sadie Ponwith, teacher

H. G. (Halvor George) Randolph, preacher and teacher

Karla Rau, assistant

John Seagard, music director

Dr. C. J. (Carl Johan) Sodergren, preacher and teacher

Eugene V. Stime, preacher and teacher

H. J. (Haakon Jonas) Stolee, preacher and teacher

Arnold (Martin Anderson) Stone, preacher and teacher

John Ylvisaker, musician and teacher

Ingrid Trobisch Youngdale, *Daily Texts*, and teacher, missionary

Caretakers: Richard Haufek, The Mattsons, Les and Ruby Larson,

The Smiths, Jerry and Jan Lang, Marvin Nysetvold, and Verney Klemm

HISTORICAL HIGHLIGHTS

1919 Samuel Miller begins the Lutheran Bible Institute

1921 Summer training sessions begin for 2 to 3 weeks

1928 Lutheran Bible Institute building is erected at 1619 Portland Avenue

1929 Samuel Miller pays off the LBI debt in August

1937 Land for Mount Carmel is purchased

1938 Mount Carmel is built as an 8 week teaching site

1959 Forty additional acres are purchased

1961 The LBI moves to Golden Valley, Minnesota

1967 The LBI becomes Golden Valley Lutheran College

1985 Golden Valley Lutheran College closes

1986 Mount Carmel has a debt of $780,000

1987 The LBI transfers property to Mount Carmel Ministries for the debt
   Proclaimers are named and organized

1992 Mount Carmel Ministries pays the debt of the bank loan

1996 First edition of *Daily Texts* is published

1997 Mount Carmel Ministries satisfies the loan with the former ALC

1997 Lodge is dedicated in July

1998 Additional sleeping rooms are built onto the Lodge

2000 Capital appeal called "M&M" raises $700,000 for Lodge debt

2003 Welcome Home Retreat House is built and dedicated

2005 Master Plan approved to expand Ministry to include a new Chapel

2006 First new cabin is built, and is called the Hans Nielsen Hauge

2007 Second and third cabins were built and called:

   The Nicolai Frederik Grundtvig cabin and
   The Philipp Jakob Spener cabin

2007 Ground-breaking ceremonies were held for the new Learning Center, the old Miller Chapel was demolished in October, and new construction began

The Re-forming of Mount Carmel

A major turning point in the story of Mount Carmel happened when the Hinderlie's were assigned to manage the camp in 1984. With the closing of GVLC, the base support system and the process for inviting guests to the camp changed dramatically. The camp was now on its own. The Hinderlie's had their work cut out for them in terms of finances and campers. The Proclaimers became the key which unlocked the door along with key personnel and new innovative programming.

The next major event came in 1992 and 1993, when a financial miracle happened which enabled the ministry to pay off a debt load somewhere around $250,000 in cash. It is a story already recounted (no pun intended) several times by other people interviewed.

The reforming process has continued to happen in many ways, not only financially and in management, not only in terms of buildings and grounds. Re-forming is what the Lord does at Mount Carmel in the lives of people. Our God reforms people. He uses the Bible preached and the Bible studied, and the Holy Spirit to make it all happen.

Many people wondered and even cried when the Board reversed the decision to re-build and refurbish the old Miller Chapel. Instead, the new recommendation came to build a new facility, which I have called the Learning Center, with a new Chapel on the upper level looking out toward beautiful Lake Carlos. The decision was correct. The Lord uses our buildings and they are necessary. But, it is the Christ-centered message—the Gospel, that gets our hearts and minds and spirit moving.

The re-forming will always continue. But, the message of Jesus Only, and the Scriptures along with the presence and power of the Holy Spirit will permeate the Mount Camel Ministries into the future.

Benediction

Now to him who is able to keep you from falling, and to make you stand without blemish in the presence of his glory with rejoicing, to the only God our Savior, through Jesus Christ our Lord, be glory, majesty, power, and authority, before all time and now and forever. Amen.

(Jude 24-25, NRSV)

My Connection

In June of 1953, my girlfriend's family, William and Vinie Westman, and their three daughters—Bernell, Vivian and Wanda invited me to a Sunday picnic at Mount Carmel. I met Bernell through her sister Vivian who had been a student at the Lutheran Bible Institute in 1952 to1953. Vivian was a Dining Room waitress at Mount Carmel for the summer. The Westmans had come up early for the worship service that was packed out with people and to visit their middle daughter.

I was also invited. The day was hot and the ceiling fans were running, with a large fan standing on the side of the chancel area.

Over the years, after our marriage in June of 1954, Bernell and I with our children—Jonathan, Rebecca, Deborah and Mary Beth, have spent a week during the summer at the camp. We missed the year's 1977 to1991 when we lived in Albuquerque, New Mexico. However, since 1993 when we moved to Coon Rapids, Minnesota, we have attended at least one week each year—usually, one of the Elderversity weeks.

Often Bernell and I stayed in cabin #29 on the far end of the Ridge of Cabins. As I walked along that ridge, I thought about the story of Mount Carmel and the great blessing it has been to people all over the world. I often wondered if anyone was writing a history of this place. The 60th year had passed by in 1998 without a lot of fanfare. The 70th year in 2008 should be celebrated with praise and jubilation.

About the Author

Orval Kenneth Moren is a retired clergy in The Evangelical Lutheran Church of America. He was a student at the Lutheran Bible Institute in 1950 and 1953. He graduated from Augsburg College, Luther Theological Seminary, and was ordained in 1960. In 1982 he earned a Doctor of Ministry from The Jesuit School of Theology Berkeley, California. He and his wife Bernell served churches in Dunseith, North Dakota, Warren, Minnesota, Duluth Minnesota and Albuquerque, New Mexico. He retired in 1991, and returned to Minnesota to reside near family.

Order Information

THE MOUNT CARMEL STORY

Postal orders: Mount Carmel Ministries
P.O. Box 579
Alexandria, Minnesota 56308

Phone orders: 1-800-793-4311

Online: www.MountCarmelMinistries.com

Book Price: $14.95